Keith & Susan,

So glad we were to connect again after all these years. I have thought about you guys often and that awareness I am lives makes it to do much more. I am grateful for your long standing friendship.

Sincerely,
Jon Rousell

7/24/09

You're *Never* Too Old

An Inspiring Autobiography of an Average Joe

Joe Rowsell

authorHOUSE®

AuthorHouse™
1663 Liberty Drive, Suite 200
Bloomington, IN 47403
www.authorhouse.com
Phone: 1-800-839-8640

© *2009 Joe Rowsell. All rights reserved.*

No part of this book may be reproduced, stored in a retrieval system, or transmitted by any means without the written permission of the author.

First published by AuthorHouse 4/1/2009

ISBN: 978-1-4389-0983-7 (sc)
ISBN: 978-1-4389-0984-4 (hc)

Printed in the United States of America
Bloomington, Indiana

This book is printed on acid-free paper.

Contents

Chapter 1: The Early Years 1
Chapter 2: College, Mission, and Marriage 26
Chapter 3: My First Child 34
Chapter 4: The Thom McAn Years 38
Chapter 5: The Real Estate Years 46
Chapter 6: Beginning My Medical Career 54
Chapter 7: My First Wife 58
Chapter 8: Multi-level Marketing 61
Chapter 9: Applying To Physician Assistant School 64
Chapter 10: Physician Assistant School 71
Chapter 11: My Dream Job 76
Chapter 12: Where New York and Idaho Meet 82
Chapter 13: Maria's Story 85
Chapter 14: Getting Engaged 95
Chapter 15: Marriage and Honeymoon 98
Chapter 16: Birth of Triplets 110
Chapter 17: The Triplet's Early Years 116
Chapter 18: Some Things Along the Way 122
Chapter 19: Losing My Dad 129
Chapter 20: Retirement 135
Chapter 21: Reflections 138

Acknowledgements

I would like to thank my wife, Maria, for writing a very personal part of her life story. It adds greatly to this book. The time and effort she spent are very much appreciated by me.

My sincerest gratitude to my good friends, Brett and Cheri King. Without their help, encouragement, and expertise, I seriously doubt this book would have ever been completed.

Thanks to my wife, Maria, and my friend, Cheri King, for finding my many mistakes and getting them corrected.

Preface

There are two reasons why I decided to write this book.

First, I wanted to write a history of my life so my children and grandchildren would have a written record of the important things in my life and not just what they heard or remembered from stories.

Second, I hope this book may become an inspiration to some who find themselves in a similar situation to the one I was in. I am sure there are many people in their middle age who have lost their jobs, are unhappy with the job they have, or have a dream that has never been fulfilled. I hope my life story may motivate them to the realization that anything is possible and you are never too old to try.

I

The Early Years

I was born on January 27, 1943. It was just over one year since the Japanese had attacked Pearl Harbor and World War II was in full swing. I was born in Lava Hot Springs, Idaho. Lava Hot Springs was a small town of about five hundred people in southeastern Idaho. It was mostly a farming community, but was unique in the fact that it had several natural hot springs. It became a tourist attraction where people came from miles around to soak in hot mineral water pools to ease their aches and pains.

I was the oldest of three children in our family. I have two younger sisters. One is four years younger than I am, and the other is seven years younger.

My mother spent ten days in the hospital after I was born. My, how times have changed! When she was discharged from the hospital, we moved to Bancroft, Idaho, about twenty miles from Lava Hot Springs. We moved there to stay with my Grandpa and Grandma Sorensen, my mother's parents, while my dad was away in the Armed Forces.

My dad was in the Air Force and stationed in Pueblo, Colorado when I was born. I was six weeks old when my dad called my mom and told her he was being shipped overseas in six weeks. He wanted her to bring me to Pueblo and spend those six weeks with him before he shipped out. We spent those six weeks with him and then he was sent to England. I didn't see him again until I was almost three years old. The European campaign ended and my dad came home on a thirty-day leave. After his leave was up, he spent time at a few different bases to get ready to go to Japan. Just before he was scheduled to leave for Japan, the atomic bombs were dropped on Hiroshima and Nagasaki and the war ended. Shortly thereafter, he was discharged from the service from Denver, Colorado. It is ironic that I have lived in Denver for the past thirty-six years. I did not know that my dad had been discharged from the service in Denver until I began doing research for this book.

After my dad was discharged from the service, he bought an old Studebaker in Denver and drove the five-hundred-plus miles to Bancroft, Idaho. He was scheduled to arrive in Bancroft in November 1945. The same day my dad was to arrive, my eighty-seven-year-old great-grandfather became lost in the mountains outside of Bancroft. My dad arrived home and, shortly afterwards the local game warden brought my great-grandfather home. He had found him wandering near a road in the mountains.

I want to spend some time now describing my parents' families to give you a sense of where I came from. First, I will tell you about my dad's family.

My dad was the youngest of six children. He had four older brothers and one older sister. They were raised on a farm three miles outside of Lava Hot Springs, Idaho. As I got older, the distance seemed to grow farther. If my dad thought my life was getting too cushy, he would remind me how far he had to walk through the snow and cold, past the cemetery, uphill both ways, to get back and forth to school.

When my Grandpa Rowsell was sixty-four years old, he sold the farm and moved to town. He and my grandma moved into a new home that he had built by himself. He took up the hobby of repairing non-working clocks. People came from all over town with their broken clocks for him to fix. I remember his back porch always being full of clocks in various stages of repair and ticking away to high heaven.

My dad's two oldest brothers, Merle and Farrell, did not serve in the war, but he and his two other brothers, Clair and Willis, did. Clair was accidentally shot in the stomach with his own gun. He survived the accident and ultimately was the last one of the six children to die. He was ninety-two years old when he died.

My dad's family in 1938
Back row left to right: Uncle Merle, Uncle Farrell, Uncle Wink (Willis)
Front row left to right: Uncle Clair, Grandma Rowsell, Grandpa Rowsell, Aunt Delsa, my dad (Joe)

My mother was the third of four children. She had two older half brothers and one younger brother. My Grandma Sorensen had a twin brother. They lived in Bancroft, Idaho in a very small house. It had a kitchen and one other room that served as a living room and bedroom. There was no hot water, no bathroom, and cooking was done on a wood stove. As small as the house was, the yard around the house seemed huge to me. There was a long path out to the edge of the yard where you would find a nice two-seater outhouse. The yard was full of trees, flowers, and wonderful places to explore and hide. There were rows and rows of strawberries, gooseberries, red and black currant bushes, apple trees, and various flowers. In the yard sat an old International pickup truck. More about this truck a little later.

All three of my mother's brothers served in the war. Her oldest half brother entered the service late and had an uneventful tour. Her younger brother was in the infantry in Italy. He was wounded in the leg while he was there. My mother's other half brother was a B-17 pilot stationed at an air base near my dad in England.

One day, my dad decided to go visit my uncle at his base. When he arrived at the base and asked to see my uncle, he was told he needed to go see the chaplain. The chaplain told my dad that my uncle had flown one of seventeen B-17s on a bombing raid over Germany. Only about half of the planes had returned. My uncle's plane was one that had not returned. The report from those who had returned was that some planes had been shot down. People were seen parachuting from those planes, but their fate was unknown. The chaplain told my dad not to say anything to the rest of the family for three weeks until they could get some definite answers as to what happened. Six weeks later, the family was notified that my uncle was officially listed as missing in action. Three months later, the Red Cross notified the family that they had found my uncle. He was in a German prisoner of war camp. He was held as a prisoner of war for the next twenty-six months until the European campaign ended. He was released and returned home to Bancroft.

After the war, my dad's next oldest brother had landed a job with the Soil Conservation Service of the U.S. Government. They were building a dam on the Portneuf River near Lava Hot Springs. They were looking for more help and my uncle got my dad a job on that project. We moved back to Lava Hot Springs and my dad worked on the dam project until it was finished. The supervisor of the dam project liked the job my dad did and offered him a full time job with the Soil Conservation Service. He gave my dad the choice of going to Grace, Idaho, a small town twenty miles from Lava Hot Springs or Montpelier, Idaho. Montpelier was the largest town in the area. It was sixty miles from Lava Hot Springs and had a population of about three thousand. Even though it was only sixty miles away from Lava Hot Springs, neither of my parents had ever been there.

My parents decided on the job in Montpelier, Idaho. My dad worked at the same job in Montpelier from then until he retired. When I was three years old, we moved to Montpelier. My parents bought a house that included all the furniture for $3,500. It was about this time that I still have some recall about our life in Montpelier.

Two months after we moved to Montpelier, my dad's next oldest brother bought a small farm in Raymond, Idaho. Raymond was an extremely small town about twenty miles from Montpelier. This turned out to become a very important event in my life and that of our families. I will talk about that later in this chapter.

Three years later, I started elementary school. There were two elementary schools in Montpelier: Washington School and Lincoln

School. Half the kids in town went to Washington and half went to Lincoln. I went to Lincoln. We had a bitter rivalry with Washington. We played frequent softball games against them. I don't remember Lincoln ever beating Washington in softball.

After I started elementary school, I spent most of my summers with my Grandma and Grandpa Sorensen in Bancroft, Idaho. I remember those summers as one of the greatest experiences of my life. I became very close to my grandparents during my elementary school years. I remember my grandma as one of the dearest sweetest people you would ever want to know. My grandpa was the greatest also. He immediately began spoiling me again. I was the apple of his eye. The oldest grandchild. In his eyes, I could do no wrong.

The yard was a veritable jungle to me. My days were spent playing with the neighborhood kids chasing and hiding from each other in this jungle wonderland.

Then there was the International pickup. I remember from the time I was too small to reach the pedals, sitting between my grandpa's legs and steering the pickup while he worked the brakes, clutch, and gas pedals. We drove all over town this way.

My grandma loved to go fishing. I don't remember her ever catching anything, but she loved to go fishing. There was a reservoir about fifteen miles away. We would pack a picnic lunch, get in the pickup, and head for the reservoir for a day of fishing. My grandpa didn't like to fish, but he was always willing to take my grandma and me fishing.

On one of our trips to the reservoir, the pickup developed engine trouble. I don't remember exactly what was wrong, but my grandpa was able to keep it running by reaching into the engine and holding something. I was big enough at that time to reach the pedals. The pickup had two hoods, one on each side. They opened independently from each other and when one side was open, it laid on top of the other hood. The headlights were mounted on top of the front fenders. My grandpa wrapped his leg around the headlight, sat on the fender and reached into the engine and kept it running while I drove the pickup for the fifteen miles down the main highway to home. I really thought I was something special to be able to do that.

My Grandpa Sorensen

My Grandma Sorensen

When I entered the fourth grade, music became part of the school curriculum. My mother had played the flute when she was in high school. She still had the flute. We couldn't afford to buy a more manly instrument, so I was stuck playing the flute. It was pretty embarrassing for a boy whose whole life revolved around fishing, hunting, and sports. I learned how to play the flute pretty well over the next three years. It was then I entered the seventh grade in junior high school. I soon found out that in junior high the band students only got gym class once a week. If you weren't a band student you got gym two times a week in seventh grade and three times a week in eighth grade. Needless to say, my flute playing days ended when I started the seventh grade.

When I was in fourth grade, my mother volunteered to teach a 4-H cooking class. That would have been fine except one of my mother's friends had a son who wanted to take the cooking class, but didn't want to be the only boy in the class. Guess who was forced to take the cooking class with him? I still remember that kid's name. The first year we learned how to make cookies. The second year was muffins. My mother got the brilliant idea for me to give a demonstration on how to make muffins at the county fair. She made me a chef's apron and a big tall stovepipe chef's hat. I did the demonstration at the county fair, against my will. Lo and behold, I won a blue ribbon for the demonstration! That was great until I found out that winning a blue ribbon entitles you to go to the state fair and give your demonstration there. I was horrified. Reluctantly, I went to the state fair, gave my demonstration, won another blue ribbon and came home. The kid that had gotten me into this mess decided not to take any more cooking classes. I was relieved I didn't have to join him in more cooking classes and could get on with more important things like fishing and sports.

Me in my baker's outfit

From my earliest recollection, I remember my dad taking me fishing. I can count on one hand the number of times my dad went fishing and didn't take me along. I am certain that in my younger years of fishing, I must have been a real pain in the butt to him. Yet he continued to take me and teach me the finer points of fishing. I am sure he spent a lot more time unsnagging me and keeping me out of trouble than he actually spent fishing. Our favorite place to go fishing was on Crow Creek. It was a beautiful stream in a beautiful valley near the Idaho-Wyoming border. We spent many days on Crow Creek fishing, laughing and listening to college football games on the radio while we ate the lunch that my mother had packed for us.

My dad also enjoyed deer hunting. He went hunting for several years before I was old enough to go hunting. One year, just before I was old enough to go hunting, my dad suddenly stopped going deer hunting. It was several years later before I found out the reason why. He had gone deer hunting with his boss. His boss saw what he thought was a deer. He fired the rifle. When they got to where the deer had been, they found a man lying dead with a gunshot wound to his neck. The investigation revealed that the man was standing behind his grey horse with his arm up on the back of the horse. The bullet my dad's boss had fired had hit the man's wristwatch, glanced off then hit the man in the throat. It was ruled an accident, but my dad never went deer hunting again.

I spent some of my summers during my later elementary school years on my uncle's farm just outside Montpelier. My uncle's two oldest children were boys, my cousins, Brent and Lynn. Brent was the older of the two. He was six months younger than me and Lynn was three years younger. We were expected to help with the farm work. We spent the days working on the farm. After the work was done for the day, we still found the energy to play football and baseball, ride horses, chase chickens and we managed to get into all kinds of trouble.

I remember, early in the mornings, helping milk the cows by hand. There were times in the winter we were milking cows in forty-below-zero temperatures. Not fun, especially when the cows were switching you with their tails and kicking over the milk buckets. During the day, we worked in the fields. I learned to drive trucks, tractors, and other farm equipment.

One fall, I was able to go on a real cattle roundup. The cattle had spent the summer grazing in the mountains. The fall was the time we rode horses into the mountains to find the cattle and herd them back to the farm so they could be fed during the winter. We left early in the morning on horseback. We rode high into the mountains, found the cattle and herded them back to the farm. What a fun day. I felt that I had become a real cowboy that day.

My uncle had a saying about the three of us boys helping him on the farm. I have never forgotten it. He said, "One boy is one boy, two boys is a half a boy, and three boys is no boy at all."

In 1955, when I was twelve, we sold our house and bought a brand new house on the other side of town. It was a three-bedroom home with an unfinished basement and a carport. We paid $10,000 for the house. The monthly payment was $55 including taxes and insurance. We also bought a brand new car: a 1955 Plymouth Savoy. The payment on the car was $27 a month. I remember my dad grumbling about what a mistake it was to have bought the new house and new car at the same time. My parents struggled with the payments for quite a while. My mother went to work during this time to help make ends meet.

1955 was the same year I started junior high school. Not long after we had moved into the new house, my Grandma Sorensen came to visit us for a while. She became ill while staying with us and ended up in the hospital. I didn't think too much of that event at the time. I was in the Boy Scout troop and we were going to scout camp for a week at the same time my grandma went into the hospital. One evening, a few days after we had arrived at scout camp, the Bishop of our church pulled into our camp. I thought he was just coming to see how we were doing. He came over and told me that my grandma had died that day. I was devastated. I got my stuff together, got into the Bishop's car and he drove me home. I cried the whole way. I couldn't believe what had happened. It was my first experience with death and the grief that accompanies it when someone you are very close to dies. My dear sweet grandma was sixty-four years old when she died.

This was also the time in my life that I began to work for money instead of for fun as I had done on my uncle's farm. Because of my dad's job, he knew all the farmers in the county. It was not difficult for him to find me jobs working on farms. I worked for various farmers for the next three summers. My job was working in the hay fields. We would go into the hay field and gather up the bales of hay, load them onto a hay wagon, take them to the hay barn, unload them, then back out into the field to get another load. It was very hard work. Some of the hay bales weighed more than I did. And all this for fifty cents an hour!

In 1957, I started high school. Along with that came football, basketball, girls, and all the other things that go along with being a high school student. You also begin pondering what you are going to do after high school. I played basketball for four years. My freshman year, I played on the freshman team. I played on the junior varsity my sophomore year. I made the varsity team my junior and senior years. We had a little better than average team, but nothing spectacular.

Football was another story. My freshman year, I was at practice one day. My parents came to the field and told me that my Grandpa Rowsell had died. I knew he had been sick, but I was not expecting him to die. I was very sad to lose him.

I finished the football season of my freshman year and, in the fall, found myself back on the field to begin my sophomore year of football. It was an exciting time for me. The school had hired a new football coach. Our team had only won two games over the past three years and they felt it was time for a change. I guess they got tired of having such a pathetic team. The man they hired was Charles "Tiny" Grant. It was his first coaching job. Despite the nickname of "Tiny," he was a giant of a man at 6'5" and 275 pounds. He had been an all-conference center at the University of Utah and had played in the NFL for a few years.

Coach Grant was also a shirttail relative of mine. My dad's brother's wife was the sister of Coach Grant's mother.

Coach Grant had a profound effect on my life, our school, and our town. He only coached us for two years but left a legacy in our town that lasts to this day. Coach Grant brought many changes to our football program. He insisted that, most of all, his players be gentlemen. There would be no more "ya" and "nah," but "yes, sir," "no, sir" or "yes, ma'am," or "no ma'am." This rule applied no matter where we were. He taught us discipline and to believe in ourselves. He taught us to be proud of who we were and always to do our very best.

On a personal level, I had my heart set on being a running back. The first day of practice, Coach Grant said he needed a quarterback to be the backup to our starting senior quarterback. He chose three or four of us to throw him some passes. I was among the ones chosen. I had no interest in playing quarterback. We each threw three or four passes to him. I purposely threw the passes at his feet, so I wouldn't be chosen. When we finished he said, "Joe, you are now a quarterback." I was extremely disappointed at the time but, as things turned out, it was the best thing that ever happened to me. I turned out to be a much better quarterback than I ever would have been a running back.

My dad wanted me to play football, I wanted to play football, but my mother was not quite so enthusiastic. I think she wanted me to cook and play the flute. My dad and I literally took her by the arms, led her to the school and forced her to sign the permission slip for me to play football.

I remember my dad showing up to watch almost every practice. My mother couldn't bear to watch. One day, my dad talked my mother into going to watch practice. Just as they arrived, someone was being carried off the field with an injury. That someone was me. I had made a tackle and caught my cleats in the grass at the time of impact. I severely twisted my left knee. We didn't know at the time what the damage was, but later found out I had torn my anterior cruciate and posterior cruciate ligaments, my medial collateral ligament, and some cartilage. That injury prevented me from playing much my sophomore year. Our team did pretty well though. We won over half our games and took second place in the district.

At the end of the school year, my parents took me to Salt Lake City, Utah, to see an orthopedic surgeon. He examined me, made the diagnosis, and said I needed surgery to repair the damage. The surgery was scheduled for the next day. My parents stayed for the surgery, but then had to go home to work and care for my two sisters. I was in the hospital for a week, by myself, 150 miles from home. When I woke from the surgery, I was in a full leg cast. It was quite a shock. The surgeon said the injury was much worse than he had suspected and that he repaired what he could. He also advised me that I probably shouldn't play football anymore. I was having none of that.

When school started again in the fall of my junior year, there I was back on the football field to try again. I was now the starting quarterback, all 5'6" and 125 pounds of me.

Me in my football uniform

Our first game was against a team from Wyoming. It was a very tough game. They won 13-7. They won the rest of their games that year and went on to win the Wyoming state championship. We won our next eight games and won our district championship. Idaho did not have a state tournament at the time so our season was finished with an 8-and-1 record. Coach Grant accepted an offer to coach a bigger school in Utah and left the end of my junior year. Everyone in the school and town was very disappointed that he was leaving.

Our new coach was Ken Peterson. He had played quarterback in college. I was excited because I felt he could probably help me to get better at my position. He was a great man in his own right and an excellent coach. He carried on many of the traditions that coach Grant had started.

We won the first six games of my senior year. We had now won fourteen games in a row. Our next game was against a big high school from Utah. They outweighed us by thirty pounds a man. We fought hard but ended up losing 7-0. They went on to win the Utah state championship that year.

We won our next game, and that set up the showdown in our last game against Preston. Preston was our district rival. The game was for the district championship. We had played one more district game than Preston, so the scenario was that we had to win or tie to win the district championship. Preston needed to win to take the championship.

It was one of the toughest football games I ever played in. Both teams wanted to win very badly. For two years, I had only played offense. The coaches didn't want me playing defense and risk getting hurt again. The problem was our starting cornerback had been injured the week before and couldn't play in this game. The coaches decided that since it was our last game, I was the best choice to fill this position for the game. I had one week to learn how to play this position on defense.

The game came down to the last five minutes. Preston was ahead 14-7. We were driving and had the ball inside the Preston ten-yard line. We ran an option play. I got hit from behind and fumbled the ball. Preston recovered. They moved the ball from their five-yard line to our thirty-yard line. Only a minute-and-a-half left. Things were looking bad for us. Preston lined up in a formation that I recognized was going to be a wide pitchout to their running back. When the ball was snapped, I ran straight ahead between their quarterback and running back. I caught the pitchout in mid air and was off to the races. I had a clear field ahead of me. Unfortunately, their running back was very fast and me, not so fast. He caught me from behind and tackled me on their five-yard line. To make a long story short, we ended up scoring a touchdown and made the extra point to tie the score at 14 with less than thirty seconds remaining. That is how the game ended. We won the district championship by virtue of the tie. I have never seen so many happy people in my life, because of a tie.

I went from being the goat to being a hero in a very short time. Thank goodness the goat part only lasted a few minutes and the hero part has lasted the rest of my life. My high school English teacher retold the story on the first day of class every year until he retired. His message to the students was that no matter how bad things look, you should never give up. He lived well into his nineties before he died. Just before he died, he was downtown with his great-granddaughter and met my mother on the street. Yes, he again relayed the story to his great-granddaughter about the quick thinking quarterback who never gave up. I suppose that might have been the last time he told that story. Every time I go back to visit in Montpelier and I see someone I know we always seem to talk about that game. I learned a valuable life lesson from that game. No matter how bad things look, you should never give up. You never know what may happen. I have had to draw on that lesson many times in my life and it has served me well.

During the summers following my sophomore and junior years, Coach Grant was hired by the city to run the city recreation program. I landed the job of being his assistant. My job was to make plaster figures for the kids to paint. I was also responsible for taking care of the softball fields. I watered them, mowed the grass, and lined the fields for the games. This job was so much better than working in the hay fields.

I did pretty well academically my first three years of high school. I made the National Honor Society my junior year. I am not quite sure what happened after that. I guess I was having too much fun my senior year to worry about such things as studying. I not only didn't make the National Honor Society my senior year, but my grades slipped to below a C average. You had to maintain a C average to get a letter in sports. I qualified for my letter in basketball, but didn't get it due to my grades.

High school was just about over for me. I still wasn't sure what I was going to do after I graduated. My football coach told me that Utah State University was interested in me playing football for them, but decided not to offer me a scholarship because they felt I was too small to compete at the college level.

We didn't have any guidance counselors at school. I had no idea about what the possibilities were in going to college. My parents strongly encouraged me to go to college but, not having much college experience themselves, they could not help me much in choosing a path.

I had really enjoyed the chemistry class I took my senior year. On a whim, I decided to go to college and major in Chemistry. I had no idea what that entailed.

At the beginning of my junior year, I met a girl who was a freshman. I fell head over heels in love with her and we dated for the next two years. It was a very different relationship because her mother had a very strict rule that she could not date the same guy two dates in a row. I guess it was her way of keeping her daughter from getting serious about anyone. It didn't work. Two teenagers in love became very resourceful. We found a myriad of ways to see each other. She would tell her mom she was going out with her girlfriends and we would meet at a pre-determined time and place. Her girlfriends would cover for her, if need be. I would also go to her house and spend time with her while her parents were at work. Her mom was a registered nurse at the local hospital.

Graduation was approaching. I asked my girlfriend to go to the graduation dance with me. You can imagine how disappointed I was when I was told that her mother forced her to accept a date with someone else that had asked her. You would think that after two years of dating and something as special as a graduation dance, her mother would have relaxed the every other date rule. Not so. I was heartbroken. We actually broke up over this, but neither one of us ever quite got over the other one.

I reinjured my knee during my senior year of basketball. It continued to be a problem. A few days before graduation, I had surgery to remove torn cartilage. My first day back at school after the surgery, I accidentally got pushed down a flight of stairs while carrying an armload of books. My knee was still very swollen and stiff. I was falling down the stairs, books flying everywhere, as I tried to catch myself on the railing. Just as I grabbed the railing, my heel caught on the edge of the step and forced me to flex my injured knee. The halls were full of students watching me fall. The dress style at the time was straight leg Levis, white socks and penny loafers. That is what I was wearing. Suddenly, I had one white sock and one red sock. Blood was running down the stairs. Everyone was staring at me with mouths wide open. I had torn open my incision all the way into my knee joint. My friends carried me to a car and drove me to the hospital. The local doctor, in phone consultation with the orthopedic surgeon, sewed me up and I spent the next five days in the hospital. You guessed it—my ex-girlfriend's mother was my nurse. Talk about rubbing it in!

A couple of days after I came into the hospital, they brought in another guy I didn't know. He was from Cokeville, Wyoming. Cokeville was a small town, just over the Idaho border, thirty miles from Montpelier. He had been in a car accident and had a broken neck. I woke one evening and saw this gorgeous blonde girl visiting him. It was his sister. We all talked for a while and, before she left, I had a date for the graduation dance with her.

The night of the graduation dance, we double dated with my cousin and his date. After I picked everyone up, we went to my parents' house for pictures and introductions. Just as we were leaving for the dance, one of my sisters said, "Why don't you drive her by Mary Lynn's (my ex-girlfriend) house to make her jealous." Talk about being embarrassed.

The parents of my date for the dance were wealthy ranchers. They owned a 10,000-acre sheep ranch in Cokeville, Wyoming. My date got my cousin and me jobs on that ranch for the summer after I graduated. We spent the summer living in a bunkhouse with the other ranch hands. It was a great summer. After each day of hard work, I would shower and get ready to go out. Soon, she would pull up in front of the bunkhouse in her Cadillac convertible. I would jump in and we were off for the evening. It has been said that all good things must end. That summer ended, along with my relationship with this girl. It was off to Utah State University to begin a new phase of my life.

2

College, Mission And Marriage

Utah State University is located in the city of Logan, Utah. It was seventy miles from my hometown. Logan was a town of about fifty thousand people, not counting the students.

I moved into my dorm room with five other guys. It was then I realized that not everyone was from small-town America. One of my roommates was from Singapore and another from Bolivia. The first few weeks of college life was a real eye opening time in my life.

I went to registration and proudly announced I wanted to major in chemistry. I was told I needed to sign up for organic chemistry and college algebra. I signed up for those two classes along with some other required courses and it was off to the races.

Utah State was on the quarter system rather than the semester system, so the terms were shorter.

I can tell you now, I was totally lost and confused from day one in my chemistry and algebra classes. It was a nightmare. I got Ds and Fs on every test throughout the quarter. My final grade in algebra was an F and a D in chemistry. I ended the first quarter with a 1.1

grade-point average. I also ended up on the wrong end of the Dean's list—academic probation.

I wondered how a former National Honor Society member could find himself in this position.

I had to re-evaluate my choice of majors. I decided to go in a more general direction and signed up for the easiest classes I could find in an effort to bring up my grade-point average. I finished the school year and got off academic probation.

I recognized my first year of college as a failure. This failure, however, had a silver lining in the fact I was able to raise my grades enough to get off academic probation.

In retrospect, I also recognized my failure in not making the National Honor Society and not getting my basketball letter. I was much too immature to recognize or admit that at the time.

I went home for the summer after the spring quarter ended. I wasn't sure what I was going to do in the future.

As you may have guessed, growing up in a small town in Idaho, I was raised in the Mormon faith. When young men in the church reached the age of nineteen, they were expected to serve a two-year mission for the church. Although not mandatory, it was expected. When I got home for the summer, I learned that many of my friends had received their mission calls. Many young men were also returning home after completing their missions. They reported their missionary experiences in church meetings. This seemed exciting to me. I also saw how much they had matured and how confident they were. Many of my friends were leaving for their missions and I decided that I wanted to go, too.

The process for going on a mission starts with the young man approaching his bishop and expressing his desire to go. He was then interviewed by the bishop and stake president to make sure he was living the rules of the church. His name was then submitted to the top leadership of the church. Soon, a letter arrived from the leadership of the church with a calling to serve a mission. It told you where you were to serve and what date you were to enter the missionary training center in Salt Lake City, Utah. I was called to serve in the Great Lakes mission that included the states of Michigan, Ohio, and Indiana. I was hoping to go to Australia but no such luck. I was happy to serve wherever they wanted me to go.

The next step was to report to the missionary training center in Salt Lake. The missionary training center experience was to last two weeks before you left to serve your mission.

I had been in the missionary training center for a little over a week when I received a phone call from my mother telling me that my Grandpa Sorensen had died. He had come to stay with us for a while before I left for the missionary training center. My family had decided to go swimming at Lava Hot Springs. On the way, they planned to stop in Bancroft and visit my Grandma Sorensen's grave. At the last minute, my grandpa decided not to go. He said he didn't feel well and wanted to stay home. When my family returned from swimming, they found my grandpa dead. He had laid down on my bed, in my bedroom, and died. He was seventy-two-years old when he died in 1962.

After my Grandma Sorensen died in 1955, my grandpa tried to live by himself in Bancroft. He did not do well there. He had diabetes and didn't take care of himself very well. My mother moved him into an apartment in Montpelier so she could take care of him. One night, he left his heating pad on high all night. He had it between his feet to keep his feet warm. It burned his ankle and he developed an ulcer there that wouldn't heal. He eventually got gangrene in his leg and had to have his leg amputated just above the knee.

It affected me deeply when he died. I wanted to go home for the funeral, but the people at the missionary training center discouraged me from doing that. They said I needed to stay with my group. They also told me our group was leaving a few days early to attend a very important conference in Canada on the way to our mission field. I reluctantly relented and did not attend the funeral. I have often regretted not going to the funeral. It was my first of several disappointments with things that happened to me in relation to the church. I realize that it was not the teachings of the church that were at fault, but some of the people in the church. More about the other disappointments later.

Fast forward twenty-eight years later to 1990. Randy Travis, a famous country music singer, released a song called "I Thought He Walked on Water." The first time I heard that song, it brought a whole slew of memories and feelings back to me. I sobbed like a baby. I felt obliged to share the words of that song with you. Due to copyright restraints, I am only able to include the first verse. You can easily access the lyrics to the whole song by going to www.randytravis.com. I am sure it will bring back many memories for some of you.

> "Wore starched white shirts buttoned at the neck
> and he'd sit in the shade and watch the chickens peck
> and his teeth were gone but what the heck
> I thought that he walked on water.

Back to 1962. We left for our destination in the mission field by train. The mission home for the Great Lakes mission was in Ft. Wayne, Indiana. This was the home of the mission president and his wife. All new missionaries stayed there for an additional week of training. I was then assigned to go to Adrian, Michigan.

My missionary companion met me at the bus depot and took me to our apartment. This was July of 1962. In December of the same year, we met the Ojeda family. They were interested in learning about the Mormon church. There were thirteen children in the family. The nine oldest children were gone from home. There were four children still at home. The oldest of these was a girl named Jeanie who was a senior in high school. The parents spoke Spanish and had a difficult time with English. They listened to our discussions but I don't think they understood much due to the language barrier. The four children however were interested in joining the Mormon church. They were baptized in January of 1963.

In February of 1963, I was transferred to Columbus, Ohio. Even though I only knew this family for two months, Jeanie and I seemed to share a strong connection.

Here are the rules set forth for young men on a mission:

1. Never be alone with someone of the opposite sex.
2. No phone calls or letters to any girls you met in the mission field.
3. No dating.
4. You must write a letter to your parents once a week.
5. It is okay for your parents to write to anyone you meet in the mission field.

The day I was to leave for Columbus, I received a phone call from Jeanie telling me she would be waiting for me until my mission was over, if I was interested.

I spent six months in Columbus, and was then transferred to Evansville, Indiana. After six months in Evansville, I was transferred again to Lafayette, Indiana. One day we came home for lunch and the whole apartment building was abuzz with something. We asked people what was going on and we were told that President John F. Kennedy had been assassinated in Dallas. It was a terrible feeling. It was a very sad time in our country's history.

My parents corresponded with Jeanie from the time I left Adrian until my mission was complete. We were able to know what each other was doing during this time. A month or two before I was released from my mission, Jeanie told her parents that she planned on marrying a Mormon boy. Her father became very angry. He beat her, threw her out of the house, and told her to never come back. She stayed with friends for a while. When my parents learned what had happened to her, they invited her to come to Idaho and stay with them. She accepted their invitation and arrived in Montpelier a month or two before I came home.

I arrived home from my mission on July 4, 1964. I remember telling my family that they really didn't need to provide all those fireworks just for me. Six weeks later, Jeanie and I were married. I was twenty-one and she was nineteen. The Mormon church encourages returning missionaries to get married soon after they get home. Looking back, I think that is a big mistake. I don't think that there are a lot of people that age who are ready for the responsibilities of marriage and children. It is a major commitment and requires a lot of mature hard work to succeed. I think that one should get an education and career before putting yourself in the situation of marriage and children. Marriage and children make getting an education a lot more difficult and sometimes nearly impossible. I certainly found that out over the next several years.

3

My First Child

A couple of weeks after we were married, we moved to Logan, Utah, and I began attending Utah State University again. It was a very difficult time. We had no money. We were trying to adjust to married life. I was attending college, but not with any real purpose or goals. I was going just because that was what you were supposed to do.

I worked weekends picking apples in a nearby orchard. It was hard work for very little money. My wife worked at an A&W root beer stand.

Three months later, we found out we were going to be parents. I was happy for that, but the pressure of school, marriage, and a child on the way was just too much for me. I dropped out of school and took a job at Walton Feed Company near Logan, Utah. I worked there for several months, and then heard about a project starting near Montpelier, Idaho. It was a huge construction project building a fertilizer manufacturing plant. The pay was great and I was able to get hired, so we moved back to Montpelier in the spring of 1965.

I was able to put a good chunk of money away while working at this job. In August of 1965, my first child was born. A girl-Lori Ann Rowsell. I was so proud. She was the first grandchild on my side of the family. My parents were thrilled and things were going pretty well. We didn't have any health insurance, so I had to pay for everything. I remember the cost of the doctor, hospital and all being $500. A small fortune back then.

While I was working at the fertilizer plant, I met a co-worker who became a friend. He was planning to go to Westminster College in Salt Lake City, Utah. He had a basketball scholarship there. We played in a summer basketball league together. He thought I was good enough to also get a scholarship. He took me to Salt Lake City and introduced me to the basketball coach. The coach watched me play and, before we left Salt Lake, I had a scholarship to play basketball at Westminster College. I enrolled in school and started with basketball practice. Before our first game, I reinjured my knee so badly it ended my season. School became very difficult, especially with a new baby that was up all night crying, night after night. I finished the first semester at Westminster College. I wasn't happy with our situation in Salt Lake and had run out of money. Another miserable failure and no idea what to do.

This was the part in my life when I had to do some serious soul searching. What do I want to do and where do I want to go and do it. After much thought and discussion with my wife and looking at our options, we decided to move to Adrian, Michigan, my wife's hometown. The plan was to work from January 1966 until college started in the fall. I had decided that I wanted to be a doctor. The University of Michigan is in Ann Arbor, Michigan. It is just a short thirty-minute drive from Adrian.

I knew I had to make some money if I was going to attend college. I planned to work as much as I could before school started in September. I ended up with three jobs. I worked in a factory from 7 am until 3 pm. I went home, showered, and went to my second job at 4 pm. That job was driving a cab from 4 pm until 10:30 pm. I was able to grab a little sleep in the cab between customers. At 11 pm, I went to my third job, at a gas station that stayed open twenty-four hours a day. I was able to get a few more minutes of sleep sitting in a chair between customers. My shift on that job ended at 6 am. Then it was back home to eat breakfast and head for my first job again. I did this five days a week and then slept most of the weekend. It was a grueling experience. I was dead tired for six straight months. That summer, I heard from the University of Michigan. I had not been accepted into school. Another failure left me in the same situation I was in before we moved to Michigan.

The only good thing about the move to Michigan was that my wife was able to reconcile with her parents. I was happy for that.

Near the end of 1966, we decided to move to Provo, Utah, so I could attend Brigham Young University. Shortly after arriving in Provo, we stopped into a Thom McAn shoe store to buy a pair of shoes for my wife. She had gotten a job at a bank next door to the Thom McAn shoe store. I recognized the man who came to wait on us and he recognized me. His dad and my dad were classmates and best friends at Lava Hot Springs High School. We had visited them often during my younger years. The two of us had played together often when we were kids. We talked about old times and he offered me a part-time job. I went to work for Thom McAn and things were looking up for the first time in a long time. I had a part-time job. My wife had a full-time job and I had been accepted as a student at Brigham Young University.

4

The Thom McAn Years

Our move to Provo, Utah, was the best decision we had made in our married life so far. I was enrolled in college part-time, had a great part-time job, and my wife was working full-time.

Soon after I started working for Thom McAn, the assistant manager left. I was promoted to assistant manager and now had a full-time job. Not long after that, the manager left and I was promoted to store manager.

It was Thom McAn's policy that all store managers were required to take a two-day aptitude test. I took the test and never gave it a second thought.

Several weeks later, I received a phone call at the store. It was the vice-president of personnel from the home office of Thom McAn in Worcester, Massachusetts. He told me I had done extremely well on the aptitude test and that I basically could write my own ticket with Thom McAn. He told me to give it some thought, tell him what direction I wanted to go, and he would make it happen.

I was in a real pickle now. I didn't know what to do. Things were going very well for us in Provo. I had plugged away at college for the past three years. I had finished ninety hours of college credits. I still had failed to go in any specific direction toward a degree. I was looking at two more years of part-time college to get a degree. I was still interested in going to medical school. I would now have to begin taking some difficult science courses. This scared me because of my miserable failure in that area during my first year of college.

We had also just bought a house. The bank had foreclosed on the previous owners and we got the house for a great price. It was a two-bedroom home with a full basement. We paid $12,500 for it.

During my time working at Thom McAn, I became close friends with the owner of a shoe repair shop. His shop was a block from the store and he did all the repairs of our damaged shoes. His name was Vern Damico. More about Vern later in this chapter.

I was very impressed with the man who was my district sales manager. I thought he had a great job with an opportunity to travel. The company provided him with a car and he made about $50,000 a year. In 1969, that was a huge amount of money. I called the vice president of personnel and told him I would like to work toward becoming a district sales manager. He said okay, but that I needed experience managing a bigger store. A huge new shopping mall had been built in the tri-cities area of Washington State. The cities were Richland, Kennewick, and Pasco, Washington. The cities were about five miles apart and the mall was built in the middle of nowhere between the three cities. Thom McAn was set to open a large store in the mall. The company wanted me to move to Washington and manage that store. The company thought it was going to be a very busy store.

Now, what to do? Should I accept the offer and begin working toward becoming a district sales manager or stay in Provo and pursue my education? The promise of money spoke louder than my discipline to finish school. I accepted their proposal and soon, we were off to Washington State. I felt pretty good about my decision, especially since the vice president of personnel told me that, if I changed my mind, all I had to do was pick up the phone, tell him I wanted to go in a different direction, and he would make that happen, too.

Back to Vern Damico. I am sure you have heard of the six degrees of separation. Here's my story about that.

Vern and his wife lived in a rental apartment. When I told him I was moving and needed to sell my house, he said he was interested in buying it. I sold the house to Vern and his wife in 1969.

Fast forward now to 1976. Vern Damico had a nephew by the name of Gary Gilmore. Gary Gilmore had been in and out of trouble his whole life, including a prison stay at Oregon State Penitentiary and a maximum-security federal prison in Marion, Illinois. In 1976, he was conditionally paroled and moved to Provo, Utah. Gilmore lived with Vern and his wife in the house that I had sold them. Vern had given him a job in the shoe repair shop to help him try to get his life on track, but Gilmore returned to his criminal ways. One July night, Gary robbed a Sinclair gas station in Orem and murdered the attendant, a man named Max Jensen. As it turns out, Jensen was from my hometown of Montpelier, Idaho. The next day, Gilmore robbed and murdered a motel manager in Provo. He was captured, tried, and sentenced to death. There are books and movies about Gary Gilmore's story. He was executed by firing squad in Utah in 1977. He was the first person executed in the United States after the death penalty was reinstated in 1976.

Back to 1969. We made the move to Washington State. The Thom McAn store opened, but it, along with the mall, was a total bust. A lot of the store managers' pay was based on a percentage of how much the store did in business. We were starving to death. I was making a lot less money than I was making in Provo. I stuck it out for six months. I couldn't see any improvement in the future of the store. I called the vice president of personnel and told him I needed to go in another direction. He arranged for me to fly to Worcester, Massachusetts. I was there for two days and was interviewed by most of the department heads in the company.

I was offered a position in the computer department as a systems analyst. Soon, we were on our way to Worcester in late 1969.

We lived in Worcester for nearly two years and hated every minute of it. The weather was miserable. The job didn't pay very much and the cost of living was very high. We found out we were expecting our second child. I got a part-time job at a local convenience store to help make ends meet. One Saturday night, just before closing, a man walked into the store, stuck a gun in my face and told me to give him all the money in the cash register. He then told me to open the safe and give him that money, too. He told me to hurry up, because if anyone else walked into the store, he would kill me. The safe was very difficult to open on a good day. My hands were shaking so badly I could barely turn the combination lock. Somehow, I managed to get the safe open and I gave him that money, too. He then instructed me to get into the back room and not come out for five minutes. I thought I was going to be killed in the back room. I came out of the back room after he had gone and called the police. The police arrived and, after an hour of being grilled by the police about why they should believe this wasn't an inside job, they let me go home. Needless to say, I went in the next day and told the manager I was not going to work there anymore. Call me chicken, but one experience like that is enough for me.

A couple of months later, I was on my way to play in a softball game. We drove through a small commercial area of town and, lo and behold, I see the man who had robbed the convenience store walking down the street. I pulled into a fire station and asked them to call the police. We drove around the area with two police cars following me. We saw the man again. I pointed him out to the police and they arrested him. I had to then go to the police station and pick him out of a lineup. He was charged with armed robbery based on my identification. I was going to testify at the trial, but his lawyer kept getting the trial postponed for one reason or another.

While all this was going on, I had talked with the vice president about how unhappy I was in Massachusetts and that I wanted to move back out west. He arranged an interview with the head of the auditing department. He said they wanted to put an auditor in Denver, Colorado, and if I wanted it, the job was mine. We were scheduled to move to Denver.

Before we moved, on June 17, 1971, my son Jason William Rowsell was born in Worcester, Massachusetts. Lori had just finished her kindergarten year of school. Nine days after Jason was born, the movers came and loaded up our stuff and headed west. I put my wife and two kids on a plane to Salt Lake City. From there, they went to my parents' house in Montpelier to stay until I arrived.

I loaded up the last of our items in an old Nash Rambler station wagon. I put our eighty-pound German Shepherd in the car and was ready to head west.

Just before I left, the police pulled up and said they needed me to testify in two days in the armed robbery trial. I told them I had no place to stay and was on my way to Idaho. I told them I would stay and testify if they could guarantee the trial wouldn't be postponed again and if they would pay for a motel room for me. They said they couldn't do that. They put a lot of pressure on me to stay. They said this guy was going to walk without my testimony. I told them my family was already gone and, if you are not willing to pay for the motel, I'm gone, too. I told them that if the guy walked, it would be their problem. The thief was so hopped up on drugs when he robbed me, I was sure he would do it again. Maybe next time, he would kill someone, but me and my family wouldn't be there if that happened. I gladly pulled out of Worcester never to look back.

My two oldest children, Lori and Jason, in 1973

We settled in Denver in September of 1971. Lori started the first grade. My job as an auditor required a lot of travel. The company provided me with a new car. I was making pretty good money, but was gone from Monday through Friday almost every week. My territory included California, Oregon, Washington, western Canada, Utah, Nevada, Arizona, New Mexico, and Texas.

In 1972, my Grandma Rowsell died. She had fallen in her yard and broke her hip. She was in the hospital for a week, and then died. She was ninety-three years old. I had now lost all four of my grandparents. I went to Idaho for the funeral.

In 1973, the company told me they were not going to keep an auditor in Denver. Most of my time was spent in California anyway and it was not cost effective to fly me there so much. They wanted me to move to California. I had spent enough time in California to know I didn't want to live there. I received an ultimatum to either move to California or be without a job. After seven years with Thom McAn, I decided I would rather be without a job than move to California. We parted company and I began wondering where my next meal was going to come from.

5

The Real Estate Years

In 1973, not long after I left the Thom McAn shoe company, I met a man named Ernie Langston. He was a real estate broker. He owned his own real estate company named Piper Realty. He thought I could do well in real estate and offered to help me get a real estate license.

I studied hard for a month or so and went to take the real estate exam. I was able to pass the exam on my first try. My new career in real estate was beginning.

I went to work for Ernie Langston at Piper Realty. About the same time, Gary Wagner went to work for Piper Realty. Soon we became very good friends.

A year later, Ernie bought a Century 21 real estate franchise and we became known as Century 21 Piper Realty.

The first year in real estate was pretty lean for me. It was tough getting started. After the first year, I did pretty well.

In 1975, Ernie decided to sell the company and move on. Gary Wagner approached me and suggested the two of us should buy the company. We put the deal together and became the proud owners of a Century 21 real estate franchise. We changed the name to Century 21 Platte Realty. I obtained my broker's license and became broker for the company.

The next three years were a booming economy in the Denver real estate market. We built the company up and had sixteen real estate agents working for us. We were making a lot of money. Things were looking very bright for the future.

I began buying houses for investment purposes. Money was very easy to borrow to accomplish this. By 1978, I had acquired thirty-three rental properties. I had a good monthly income from the rent from these properties.

In 1975, I became good friends with Phil and Terry Ray. They were the parents of five children: Darin, Brian, Marilee, Rachelle, and Janel. The Ray family became a very important part of my life. Our friendship has lasted until this very day. As you go through life, many friendships come and go. Few are long lasting. Someone once said that in life you can count on one hand the number of true friends you have. The Ray family and Gary Wagner are two that I can certainly count on.

In 1977, the Ray family moved to a home across town. I sold them that house and bought the house they were selling to make the move. It was a large house near a lake. I paid around $50,000 for the house. The average price of a house in Denver at that time was around

$25,000. We were living pretty high on the hog. I bought a Lincoln Continental and had a mobile phone installed. I was the epitome of success. I refused to think that it would ever end.

I arranged a fishing trip to the Great Slave Lake in the Northwest Territories of Canada. I took my dad and my son Jason, who was eight at the time, for a weeklong stay on Brabent Island. We flew to a small town near Brabent Island. We then took a floatplane to the island. The pilot of the floatplane was very young. He looked like he still might be in high school. Needless to say, we were a little nervous about the trip. We arrived at Brabent Island in one piece however. We had our own cabin to sleep in. There were no telephones or TVs on the island. The sun was up about twenty hours a day. It was a wonderful time. Three generations of guys fishing for a week. By the time the week was up, we were begging the fish to stop biting. We were all dead tired from catching so many big fish.

During this time, my dreams of going to medical school came to the forefront again. I began to position myself to accomplish this. I enrolled at the University of Colorado at Denver and began taking the science courses I needed for a degree with the hopes of getting in to the University of Colorado medical school. I was attending school on a part-time basis and working in real estate full time. I was also doing some volunteer work in the emergency room at Denver General Hospital. It was also known as the Denver Knife and Gun Club. The emergency room saw a lot of major trauma. Stabbings and gunshot wounds were commonplace. I saw it all. I decided that emergency medicine was what I wanted to do. I was about thirty-five years old at the time, and I figured this might be my last shot to see my medical school dreams come true.

I sat down and evaluated my financial situation to see if I could afford to raise a family and go to medical school at the same time. I figured out that with the income from the rental houses I would have about $3,000 a month in spendable income. That was a lot of money at the time—more than enough to accomplish my dream.

During this same period, I was asked by my church to serve as the bishop of our congregation. A bishop in the Mormon church is equivalent to a pastor in the protestant faith or a priest in the Catholic faith. I accepted and served as bishop for the next two years. Among my many duties as bishop, I performed several marriages and conducted several funerals. I had to be at the church very early on Sunday mornings for pre-service meetings. That left my wife to get the kids ready for church and make it to the church on time. The problem was that she was nearly always late. One day, she was running especially late. She brought the kids to church, but hadn't had time to feed them breakfast. During the passing of the sacrament, bread and water, it was a very quiet and reflective time. I am sitting on the stand conducting the meeting. Suddenly, I hear my son Jason say in a loud voice "I don't want bread. I want pancakes." Everyone in the congregation broke up laughing while I sat there rather embarrassed.

I was doing my volunteer work at Denver General one evening. My eight-year-old son Jason was playing in a little league baseball game. My wife and fourteen-year-old daughter Lori were at the game. The baseball fields were just down the block from our house. Lori was walking along the edge of the street with two of her girlfriends when a car came speeding around the corner and hit Lori from behind. I was later told that the impact knocked her 15 to 20 feet into the air. She came back down and landed on the hood of the car. A friend called me at the hospital and told me what happened. I was told an ambulance was taking her to a hospital that was fifteen miles away from where I was. I left Denver General immediately and headed for the hospital where they were taking her. I arrived at that hospital and she hadn't arrived yet. I was freaking out. Just a few days before at Denver General, I had seen a brother and sister brought into the emergency room. They had been hit by a car in an accident very similar to Lori's. I watched them both die from their injuries. I kept looking out the window of the hospital, waiting for the ambulance. Soon, I caught sight of the ambulance. No lights or siren. It was moving at a very slow speed. My heart sunk. I feared the worst. I thought Lori had died on the way and there was no reason to hurry. When she arrived, I was relieved to find out that she was alive and awake. She had a large cut on her head and there was a lot of blood everywhere. She had a lot of scrapes and bruises everywhere. She spent a couple of days in the hospital and was terribly sore for a couple of weeks. I was extremely grateful she wasn't hurt worse than she was.

Things really began to unravel for me in 1979. Gary Wagner decided to sell his half of the company. I bought him out and became the sole owner. Shortly after I bought Gary out, the real estate market took a huge downturn. Interest rates reached a historic high of around 20%. No one could afford to buy a home at that rate. There was no way to make any money. I had a large overhead with the real estate company. Soon, all my salesmen had gone on to pursue other careers. I had $250,000 out on short-term notes. Due to the economy, the bank wouldn't renew the notes and called them due. The rental market went south also. I couldn't get enough rent to make any money, let alone cover the mortgage payments. Before it was all over, I had to file for business and personal bankruptcy. I lost the real estate company, all thirty-three of the rentals, the house I lived in and both my cars. This was truly the low point in my life.

I was released as bishop of the church and suffered a severe spiritual depression as well as being depressed from losing everything else.

Another big disappointment in the church came at this time, too. My insurance agent, who was also a high-ranking member of the church, got into financial trouble as well. He started keeping my premium payments for his own use instead of sending them into the company. A few months later, the insurance company cancelled all my insurance for non-payment. I called them and told them I had been making the payments. They investigated the agent, found out what he was doing, and fired him.

I quit volunteering at Denver General, quit going to school and fell into a deep depression for the next two years. My medical school dreams were dashed. I didn't know what I was going to do. I felt completely worthless. It was very difficult for me to get out of bed in the mornings. My daughter, Lori, was in high school. She was a cheerleader. I could barely provide food for my family, let alone anything else. My son, Jason, was still in elementary school. His needs were not as great as Lori's and I figured he would not be as affected by my troubles as Lori. I felt horrible that I couldn't provide my family with a decent way of life.

To make things worse, my cousin Brent, from the farm in Raymond, Idaho was diagnosed with melanoma. He had multiple surgeries and fought the disease for two years. He finally succumbed to this deadly form of skin cancer at age 38. This added to my depression. We were very close while we were growing up. It seemed the whole world was falling down around me. This whole period was a gigantic failure and disaster—the biggest of my life.

My wife and I began drifting apart. She looked at me as someone who couldn't support his family. I am sure I wasn't the easiest person to live with during this time.

6

BEGINNING MY MEDICAL CAREER

After we lost everything, we had to find a place to live. We found a home to rent and moved in. My parents helped me buy an old car to get around in. The time had come for me to pick myself up, dust myself off, and quit feeling sorry for myself. I remembered the lesson I had learned from high school football. Never give up and all that. I had a family to take care of.

I delivered newspapers and worked at a self-serve gas station to try to make ends meet. I began searching for some kind of meaningful job that I could turn into a long-term career. I did not have a college degree. That made finding a good job very difficult. Whenever I applied for a job, no one wanted to hire me because I had been in real estate. They were concerned that when the real estate market got good again, I would leave and return to real estate. No matter how hard I tried to convince them that I wasn't going to do real estate anymore, they didn't believe me. I couldn't find a decent job anywhere.

I went to work for another member of our church. He owned a fence company. All outward appearances seemed like he was doing extremely well. He owned his own business, drove fancy cars, and lived in a very pricey home in an upscale area of the city.

I hadn't worked for him for very long when he approached me and said he really liked the job I was doing for him. He said he had an opportunity for me to make some extra money if I wanted to. He said he had fallen into a deal where he could buy trainloads of lumber for a super price. He could sell some of the lumber to other fence companies and realize a very good profit. If I could find some investors and raise some money to help him buy the trainloads of lumber, he would pay me a nice commission on the money I raised. The investors would realize a very nice profit also in a short period of time.

I was able to get my parents and some other friends to invest. It worked great for a while. I was making a good commission and the investors were getting a nice return in a short period of time. As time went on my investors were willing to invest more and more money.

Then things started going badly. There was one excuse after another about problems on the other end of the deal. I began to smell a rat. I did some investigating and realized that he was running a Ponzi scheme and using the money to pay for his extravagant life style. My parents, along with my friends, were at risk of losing a lot of money. I was sick to my stomach that I had been taken advantage of like that. I was even sicker that my friends and parents were going to lose their money. I let everyone know what was going on. I suggested we get an attorney. We met with the owner of the fence company and his attorney. It was a knock down drag out session. In the end, he relented and everyone got their money back. I quit working for him. Another big disappointment from a supposedly good member of the church. He got prosecuted, lost his house, and part of his sentence was that he could never own a business in Denver again. I guess he got what he deserved.

I was out of a job again. Still depressed, with nothing I could foresee giving me any sign of hope.

My wife had talked to someone who had gone to Parks College (a trade tech) and had learned to become a travel agent. My wife thought she might like to do that. She asked me to pick up a catalog from Parks College, so she could see what she needed to do to become a travel agent. I picked up the catalog for her, but I don't think she ever looked at it. I did though. I found out they had a medical assistant program. That piqued my interest. I found out that medical assistants didn't make a lot of money, but earned enough to pay the rent and put food on the table. I decided I would try to do that and maybe work real estate part time. Between the two things, I might be able to provide a decent living for my family. I went to the college to find out more. When the school found out how little money I had made over the past couple of years, they said I could qualify for a Pell grant. I qualified for the grant, so I signed up for the twelve-month course.

I finished the program, passed the certification exam and got a job at the Arvada Emergency Center. It was a walk-in urgent care center. We were open from 7 am to 11 pm, 365 days a year. It was a great job. I had finally made it into the medical field, although not exactly as I had dreamed of.

One of the classes I took at Parks College was a law and ethics class. There was one small paragraph in the textbook about Physician Assistants. I had never heard of a Physician Assistant. I approached one of my instructors and asked what they knew about Physician Assistants. She told me she thought the University of Colorado Health Sciences Center had a Physician Assistant program and that I should go there and get more information.

I went to the Health Sciences Center and picked up an application package for the Physician Assistant program. This event turned out to be a major turning point in my life. More about that in a couple of chapters. I want to take the next two chapters to fill in some gaps with some important things in my life.

7

My First Wife

My marriage started out pretty well. As the years went by, my wife became more and more manipulative. When she wouldn't get her way, my life would become extremely miserable for the next several days. I soon learned that it was much easier to give in to her than to pay the price I would have to pay if I didn't give in to her. I didn't realize it at the time, and didn't know what it was, but I became an enabler. I allowed her or enabled her to manipulate me. The longer we were married, the more she manipulated me. I allowed it just to keep peace in the family.

Looking back now, I don't think she was ever happy. I seriously doubt if she ever really loved me.

She always managed to spend a little more money every month than we made. It didn't matter how much or how little we made, she always managed to spend a little more. I allowed her to do that to keep peace. As a consequence, we were in debt the whole 29 years we were married.

She was very often sick. She was always so sick, she couldn't get out of bed. Sometimes, she would be in bed for several days at a time.

She never had any symptoms of anything. She just said she was sick. I always had to call her boss and tell them she was sick and wouldn't be in to work.

She was never able to keep a job for any length of time. The longer she worked at a job, the more often I had to call in sick for her. I soon recognized a pattern. The longer she held a job, the more often she became sick, until finally, she would claim she was just too sick to work anymore. I would have to call in and quit her job for her. She would or could never do that for herself. This pattern repeated itself over and over again throughout our married life. The longer we were married, the worse it got.

Our housing situation followed the same pattern. The longer we lived in a house, the more antsy she got and wanted to move. During the 29 years of our marriage, we moved a total of 39 times. We moved 20 of those times after we moved to Denver in 1971. We just moved from house to house in the same town.

I think she was just so unhappy that she thought a new job or a new house would make her happy. It never did.

While I was working at Arvada Emergency Center, I became good friends with Dr. David Olsen. As I learned more about medicine, it became increasingly clear to me that my wife was suffering from some kind of depression. Dr. Olsen and I convinced her to see a physician who could possibly help her. She agreed to do that.

The physician she saw figured out the problem. He prescribed some medicine for her and soon, she had improved greatly. She seemed happier and better able to cope with things. A lot of people with this disorder stop taking their meds after they start feeling better. That happened with my wife. She would get to feeling better, stop taking her meds, and soon revert back to the same unhappy sickly person. I would talk her into taking the medicine again. She would improve, then stop her meds, and get bad again. It was a real roller coaster ride for the next several years.

8

Multi-Level Marketing

It has been said that the definition of insanity is doing the same thing over and over and expecting different results. That has been my experience with the many multi-level marketing ventures I have tried.

Multi-level marketing is a marketing concept that has been around for many years. The idea behind this concept is to come into the business under a sponsor. The sponsor then receives a percentage of your sales for bringing you into the company. You then try to sponsor as many people into the business as you can. You then get a percentage of their sales. This continues to go down the line for several levels with a smaller percentage for you the further down the level is. The idea is to build as big of an organization as you can and receive money from everyone below you in your organization. The more business your organization produces, the more money you make. At least that is the theory.

I have tried many different multi-level marketing products over the years. The products were different and the pay schedule was a little different, but the concept was the same.

My first experience with multi-level marketing was many years ago in Provo, Utah. The company marketed Figurette Bras. These were the newest thing in shaping bras for women. As with most multi-level marketing companies, you had to buy a sales kit and inventory to begin. This included a huge suitcase full of bras in different sizes and some information on how to become successful in this business. I was so successful in this business that I was unable to make enough money to even pay for the kit and inventory I had purchased. I ended up giving the bras away to friends and relatives. Imagine that, I had found another way to fail.

Almost all of the multi-level marketing companies get you interested in the same way. They hold up a few people in their company that have done very well and become wealthy. They don't tell you about the thousands of people who have gotten involved and not even made enough money to pay for their original investment.

The chances of making a lot of money in a multi-level marketing company are probably comparable to a high school athlete making it big in professional sports. It happens to only a very few.

Over the years, I have tried many multi-level marketing plans. The result has always been the same. I have tried Holiday Magic cosmetics, waterless cookware, Tupperware, A.L. Williams, an insurance and investment company, Pre-paid legal services, and probably a few more that I can't recall. Insanity—same thing over and over while expecting different results.

I finally decided that multi-level marketing was a waste of time and money. I wasn't going to get involved anymore. After many years of not being involved in any multi-level marketing plans, one more came along that I felt was a "can't-miss" opportunity. I was in the medical field at the time and the product was some natural health product offered by Rexall drug company. It seemed different, and I felt it would be a natural for me since I was already in the health care field. Fooled again. Years later, I still have Rexall products sitting around all over my house. Same failure, more insanity.

9

Applying To Physician Assistant School

I went to the University of Colorado Health Sciences Center in late 1983 or early 1984 and picked up an application package for the Physician Assistant program for the class that was to begin in June 1985. I had about a year to get the application filled out and turned in before the application deadline.

I reviewed the information I had gotten from the school. The only thing in the information that gave me any encouragement at all was that you needed only ninety hours of college credit to qualify. I had enough hours of college credit, but lacked a few required courses. I would need to take three more classes to fulfill those requirements. I still needed organic chemistry, microbiology, and a child development class. I figured I could do that so I enrolled at Front Range Community college and began taking classes.

There were many things in the information that gave me great discouragement. One was that you needed at least a 2.5 grade-point average. My cumulative grade-point average for my college grades was a 2.3. Most of my college classes had been taken fifteen to twenty years ago. I would be forty-two years old by the time the class I was applying for would begin.

The application itself was very complicated and tedious. I would need to get several letters of recommendation. There were many essay questions I needed to answer. They involved subjects that I had very little or no experience in.

It was a very frustrating year for me as I worked on the application. I would begin working on the application, but quickly get discouraged because of my previous grades and the length of time since my college classes had been taken and my age at the time. I knew I would be competing with recent college students who were much younger than myself. I would throw the whole mess into a drawer and think, "Why am I doing this? I don't have a prayer of getting accepted." Then, a while later, I would take it out of the drawer, work on it a while, get discouraged all over again and throw it back in the drawer. I wanted to just forget about it, but I never could quite get it off my mind. This process went on for nearly a year. I finally finished the application and turned it in the day before the deadline.

The secretary at the school gave me more information about the program and the application process. This discouraged me even more. She told me they had over 160 applications for twenty positions in the class. The process was to review all of the applications. Half of them would be eliminated and half would receive an interview. Those who made it to the interview would get a letter from the school in December 1984. The interviews took place in January 1985 and the letter would tell you when your interview was scheduled. I remember thinking, "Well, I turned in the application, but that will be the end of that. At least, I tried."

Imagine how surprised I was when I received a letter giving me an interview date! I became more hopeful, but still had serious doubts about getting accepted.

I went to my interview in January of 1985. The interview process lasted for two days. The first day, four different people interviewed me for two hours each. The second day consisted of a group interview. There were six applicants who were interviewed by a panel of six people. After the interview process was over, I went home feeling more convinced that I didn't have much of a chance to get accepted.

A month later, I received a letter from the Physician Assistant program at the University of Colorado Health Sciences Center that changed my life. I had been accepted into the program with the following conditions: a $200 deposit to hold my place and I had to complete the three classes I was taking with a C grade or better. I was as excited as I had ever been in my life. I was filled with excitement, disbelief, anxiety, and apprehension, all at the same time. I still wondered if I had what it would take to make it through the program. I didn't know, but by golly, I was going to try as hard as I could!

I finished taking the three classes I needed to meet the conditions of my acceptance into the program. I got two Bs and a C. I somehow scrounged up and sent in the $200. All that was left to do was wait for school to begin in June of 1985.

School would begin the first week of June. There was a two-day orientation the week before school started. During the first day of orientation, I received a big shock. We were told that the program was very intense and that you couldn't possibly work, even part time, and make it through the program. I had a full-time job as a medical assistant and needed to work to take care of my family. There was no way I could make it through the program without working full time. I decided to keep my mouth shut about my job and do what I had to do to get through. I arranged for a student loan to pay the tuition and books. I was able to coordinate my work schedule and school schedule, so there wouldn't be any conflict. My supervisor at the Arvada Emergency Center was very helpful in arranging my work schedule to accommodate my school schedule. School was Monday through Friday, but we got out early on Wednesday afternoons. I was able to arrange my work schedule to work from 3 pm to 11 pm on Wednesdays. I then worked from 7 am to 11 pm on Saturday and Sunday. It was a grueling schedule, but I was determined to make it work.

Needless to say, I was not at home very much. When I was home, I was trying to keep up with my schoolwork. My wife and I drifted even farther apart during these difficult three years.

The first year of school was 90% classroom work and 10% clinical work. The second year was 50% classroom and 50% clinical. The third year was the internship year and we rotated through many different clinics. School was a wonderful experience for me. After the first year of the program, I received a Bachelor of Science degree from the University of Colorado. Finally, after twenty-five years of attending college off and on, I received a college degree. I was so happy and proud. After the third year, I completed a research project and received a Master of Medical Science degree from the University of Colorado. I couldn't believe it. I had accomplished more than I ever really thought I would or could!

The Physician Assistant program had a heavy emphasis on pediatrics. Two weeks after I started school, my daughter, Lori, gave birth to my first grandchild. Her name is Jamie. It was very convenient for me to have a granddaughter born at this time. I had my own personal baby to practice my exams on. She was probably the most examined baby in history.

School was finally over. I had graduated from the program with a B average. I had passed the national certification exam and was ready to go out and find a job as a Physician Assistant. An unbelievable dream come true! I continued to work as a medical assistant while I looked for a Physician Assistant job.

It was during my three years of PA school that I experienced the last of my disappointments with people in the Mormon church. Some close friends of ours had a brother who was an attorney in Arizona. He was also a bishop in the Mormon church. Our friendship with these people had lasted for fifteen years. We had met their brother several times. As an attorney, he represented an Indian tribe in Arizona. He had worked out a deal with them to build a large shopping center and RV park on the corner of their reservation. He was looking for investors to help finance the project. He got his parents and most of his brothers and sisters to invest in the project. It sounded like a great deal, but I didn't have any money to invest. I discussed the deal with my friend, Dr. Olsen. He thought it sounded good, too. He invested $9,000 and loaned me that same amount to invest in the project. The attorney even hired two of his siblings to work for him on the project. Several months went by and the reports we got said things were moving along nicely. As more time passed, his family became suspicious that things were not going along so nicely. They got in their car and drove from Denver to Arizona to see for themselves what was going on. They discovered that there was no such project in the works and that he had been disbarred two years earlier. He had been indicted by the state attorney general for fraud and was due to go to court. He was convicted. He was released pending his sentencing hearing. He didn't show up for his sentencing. His family or anyone else that we know of has ever heard from him since. It is like he just disappeared from the face of the earth. What happened to him remains a mystery to this day.

10

Physician Assistant School

The three years I spent in Physician Assistant school were amazing. The volume of material that we had to learn was staggering. The time we spent in various clinics was incredibly interesting. The whole process was simply magnificent. I entered Physician Assistant school not feeling like I was a very educated person. I left Physician Assistant school feeling very well educated and ready to go to work practicing medicine. It wasn't long after I started working that I felt somewhat uneducated again. I soon realized that the three years of Physician Assistant school had only prepared me to begin learning the practice of medicine. I soon learned that all the book learning I had done was helpful, but the problem was the patients hadn't read the books. They didn't always present with the same neat set of symptoms that were described in the books. There were usually other issues involved in every case and sometimes it was very difficult to sort all of that out.

In spite of feeling somewhat lost and dumb for a while, I loved the work. I loved taking care of patients and I loved the fact that everyday was a new learning experience.

Not all things in the practice of medicine are fun and exciting. I want to share a few experiences with you that were gut-wrenching to me. Some of them were so difficult that I sometimes wondered if I had made the right choice in going into medicine.

All of the following experiences happened to me while I was still in Physician Assistant school.

One of our first year clinical rotations was to work in the pediatric clinic at University Hospital. We each obtained two or three expectant mothers from the OB clinic to follow through the last few months of their pregnancy. We went to the delivery of their babies and then took care of the babies in our pediatric clinic until we graduated or the family stopped using our clinic. Just an interesting sidelight here. When we started to work in the pediatric clinic we were introduced to the regular staff of the clinic. One of the medical receptionists that I was introduced to was John Denver's mother. She had worked at the clinic for many years. Working in this clinic was a wonderful experience for the most part.

One of the families that I was taking care of was not doing very well. The two kids were not gaining weight like they should and had several other problems. After several visits, it became apparent that these parents were neglecting and possibly abusing these children. I got social services involved and, before long, the children were removed from the home and placed in foster care. I know we did the right thing for the children, but it was very difficult to see a family being torn apart like that. I felt sorry for the parents and I am sure they were not very happy with me.

In my third year of Physician Assistant school, one of the rotations I did was in the Neonatal Intensive Care Unit at Denver General Hospital. I spent a month there. The Neonatal Intensive Care Unit is where premature babies go as well as babies with serious health problems. During this month, I saw some really horrible things. While I was there, one baby was born with a genetic syndrome. The child was born without most of his brain. He had a brain stem that allowed him to breathe and keep his heart beating. His head was very small and pointed on top. He had no nose. He just had a hole in his face where his nose should have been. This poor child had no chance of living a normal life.

There was another baby born that had a very rare metabolic syndrome. As I recall, there were only six reported cases of this syndrome in medical history. The syndrome caused this baby to suffer from a constant state of seizures. This baby was not expected to survive very long, but was still alive when I finished my rotation.

I saw several babies that were born with fetal alcohol syndrome, a problem caused when the mother consumes alcohol during her pregnancy.

There were many babies born who were addicted to cocaine, heroin, and other illicit substances. These babies suffered from withdrawal symptoms and were very irritable. Imagine going through drug withdrawal as a baby because of your mother's drug addiction. I saw countless other things during that month that were really heartbreaking.

Once, during my rotation at The Children's Hospital in the Intensive Care Unit, I witnessed something that nearly made me give up my dream of working in the medical field.

A child, about a year-and-a-half old, had been at his grandmother's house. The child had discovered a bottle of oil of cloves that his grandmother had used to relieve a toothache. Somehow, the child managed to open the bottle and started to drink it. Oil of cloves is very strong. When the child drank some, it caused him to gasp and he sucked the oil of cloves into his lungs. As a result, he ended up in the Intensive Care Unit on a ventilator. The child developed pneumonia and was very sick. Tests were done after a month of being on the ventilator and no response from the child. It was determined the child was brain dead and only being kept alive by the ventilator. The parents had to make a decision as to what to do. If they removed him from the ventilator, he would die in just a few minutes. The parents decided to remove him from life support. I was there when they sat the mother in a rocking chair and gave the baby to the mother to hold. The rest of the family gathered around the chair as the doctors removed the life support equipment. It took several minutes for the child to finally quit breathing and die. I stood there watching with tears streaming down my face. My heart felt like it was going to break. I wasn't sure how many of these experiences I could go through and still like being in medicine.

I thought about it long and hard, but decided to stick it out. I remembered all the good things about medicine. All the people that we were able to relieve their suffering and cure their illnesses. There are just times when there is nothing you can do to save people in spite of all the knowledge and technology we have. It is obvious to me that the decision of who lives and who dies does not rest with anyone here on earth, but with a higher power.

11

My Dream Job

I began looking for a job in June of 1988, after I graduated from Physician Assistant school. I was now forty-five years old. I found a couple of temporary jobs filling in for some pediatricians who were going on vacation. It was a good experience for me, but I still didn't have a full-time job.

I read a help wanted ad in the newspaper. There was a full-time job offered by Kaiser Permanente, a large HMO in Colorado. I applied for the job. After two interviews, I was offered the position as a Physician Assistant in the emergency room at St. Joseph Hospital. My dream of working in an emergency room had come true. I was walking on cloud nine. I had to keep pinching myself to see if it was real.

I had been at work for two hours, on my first day, when I received a phone call from my daughter, Lori. She had gotten divorced from her first husband and had met Kurt Minter, a man she had become serious about. They had gotten engaged and went to Rifle, Colorado, for the weekend to meet Kurt's parents. My granddaughter, Jamie, was with them. Kurt's parents had an old dog. The dog was half German Shepherd and half Wolf. The dog weighed about one hundred pounds and Jamie weighed twenty-five pounds. Jamie walked down the stairs in the morning and Lori heard the dog growl and Jamie scream. The dog had been sleeping and Jamie bent down to hug the dog. It startled the dog and the dog bit Jamie on the face and neck. It was a severe bite. Jamie's left ear and left side of her face were torn away. She had two deep puncture wounds over her spine behind her neck. She was bleeding profusely. Kurt and Lori wrapped her up in a blanket and started the eight-mile drive to the nearest hospital. The emergency room doctor checked her out and immediately called a plastic surgeon in Glenwood Springs, about thirty miles away. He immediately drove to Rifle and Jamie was prepared to go to the operating room. The plastic surgeon spent five-and-a-half hours in the operating room putting her face back together. She spent the next five days in the hospital after the surgery. Fortunately, she did not suffer any permanent damage except for the scar on the left side of her face.

The minute I got the call, I left for Rifle and stayed with Jamie until she was released from the hospital. I wasn't sure I would still have my job when I returned, but the powers that be at Kaiser Permanente were very gracious and I was still employed.

My job in the emergency room was very interesting and exciting. As much as I had learned in school and during my internship, it didn't take long to recognize how much I still didn't know. The real education you get in medicine comes after you finish school and begin working at a real job. The doctors and other physician assistants that worked there were absolutely fantastic in teaching me what I needed to know to be successful at my job.

I took care of all kinds of patients with all kinds of problems. It was amazing how much more I learned in a short period of time. Before long, I was doing things that I didn't ever believe I would be doing. I was suturing people with all kinds of lacerations. I repaired tendons that had been lacerated. I was straightening out arms and legs that were crooked because of broken bones. I was putting casts on fractured extremities. I learned how to read X-rays, make the diagnosis, and treat the problem. I saw people with abdominal pain, chest pain, strokes, very sick babies, and much more. I did spinal taps on sick babies and adults to make sure they didn't have meningitis. It was all amazing. I loved the work and soon became a workaholic. I couldn't get enough. I was working about seventy hours a week and relished every minute of it.

The main job of a physician assistant at Kaiser Permanente was to take care of the trauma patients. I became very good at repairing lacerations. Many of the people I worked with began asking for me to take care of them and their families when they got hurt. I was very honored that people who saw my work would ask me to take care of their families. That is one of the highest forms of respect you can get.

One thing that always saddened and amazed me about working in the emergency room was the horrible things that people do to each other and to themselves. I saw many people with mental illness in one form or another. Some of these people would self mutilate. They would cut themselves with knives, burn themselves with cigarettes, and various other forms of harmful behavior.

I removed every kind of foreign body imaginable from every body orifice there is. In some ways, that was the most amazing thing of all.

I saw many people who were addicted to drugs and/or alcohol. Many of them were in extremely bad shape. Many of them died.

There were many people who attempted suicide. Some succeeded and some failed. I have been through some very rough times in my life, but never thought things were so bad I wanted to take my own life.

I saw parents bring their children into the emergency room because the child was unresponsive. The stories were all similar. They fell off the couch or I'm not sure what happened. Often after examining the child, it was discovered that the child had been beaten. They had multiple broken bones in various stages of healing. Some were shaken so badly that it caused bleeding in the brain. Many of these children didn't survive. Those who did were usually left with some brain damage. They were taken away from the parents and placed in the care of Social Services who found foster homes for these kids.

I remember one man who came into the emergency room. He had a very bad infection in his scrotum. There were sutures in the scrotum holding an incision together. The man told me he felt like he had too much sex drive. He said he had a veterinarian friend of his remove one of his testicles to cut his sex drive in half. I didn't believe the story because I couldn't imagine any veterinarian risking his career to do such a thing. Finally, the truth came out. His wife had removed one testicle, on their kitchen table, without anesthesia. The testicle had been put in a jar and was in the refrigerator. They had saved it in case they wanted to put it back in at a later time. Unbelievable as it may seem, it is a true story.

I saw many people with psychiatric problems. A lot of them had enablers as partners. That is what I had been with my wife. I learned that being an enabler does not help the mentally ill person. I decided that I had had enough of doing that. I stopped being an enabler and started putting my foot down. As soon as I started doing that, I came home from work one day and my wife had all her things packed and informed me she was leaving me. We had been married for twenty-eight years at the time she left. As much as you know that it is for the best, it is still very difficult to go through a divorce. She left in the summer of 1992 and filed for divorce in December. Our divorce became final in October of 1993.

We were deeply in debt, as usual, at the time of our divorce. I was left owing $80,000. I had to continue paying her health insurance, pay for her car, her attorney fees and give her $600 a month in alimony. She walked away not owing anyone a dime. I was ordered to pay her the $600 a month for 17 years until she turned sixty-five or until she remarried.

My son, Jason, and I lived together after my wife left. He was twenty-one at the time. One day, a year after our divorce was final, Jason told me that she was going to get married again. She wanted him to come to the justice of the peace and watch her get married. He didn't want to go, but I told him he had to go to make sure she signed all the papers and really got married. He said he would do that. He came home and assured me that she was now married. The alimony stopped and saved me over $100,000.

Soon, she and her new husband were in debt up to their eyeballs and I was nearly out of debt and making very good money.

I was fifty years old and single again. It was a scary time. What should I do now? I hadn't dated since I was in high school. Times had changed drastically since then. I didn't even have a clue how to go about dating in this day and age.

Between the time I graduated from Physician Assistant school and got divorced, my daughter, Lori, presented me with two grandsons. Chase was born in 1991 and Colin was born in 1993. I was able to witness the birth of both of my grandsons.

12

Where New York And Idaho Meet

A few months after my wife left, it became obvious to me that our marriage would end in divorce. I was sad for that, but at the same time, I felt a great sense of relief to be out of the marriage.

I decided it was time to get on with my life. I wanted to start dating, but was a little apprehensive about doing that. The last date I had was thirty years ago in my last year of high school. I knew times had changed a lot since then and I wasn't sure how to go about dating again.

It wasn't long before my anxiety about dating again disappeared. As soon as it became known that I was "on the market," I had more dates than I could handle. Many ladies began asking me for dates. I asked many other ladies for dates. My social life was booming. It did wonders for my ego, although it seemed strange that women would ask me out. The last time I had dated, it was taboo for a girl to ask a boy for a date. We even held one dance a year where it was okay for the girl to ask the boy. It was called the Sadie Hawkins dance.

I was having a ball. I guess I was trying to make up for the lost time because I got married so young and didn't ever have a chance to date after high school.

Over the next two years, I had a few short-term relationships and a lot of one or two time dates. I had no intention of doing anything else for a long time.

That all changed in the summer of 1993. I was sitting at the nurses' station doing some paperwork. A young, beautiful, tall, thin girl walked by the nurses' station. She had on a white lab coat and employee nametag. I had never seen her before. I was smitten immediately. I asked my friend, "Who in the hell is that?" He told me she was some girl who had just started working in the emergency room. She worked in the lab. She was from New York and was married, so I should just forget about her.

Over the next few months, our paths crossed several times and we got to know each other a little better. Her name was Maria and she was born in Brooklyn, New York. She moved to Long Island when she was seven and had lived there all her life. She was not happy to be in Colorado.

Soon, the talking turned into flirting and we became closer and closer.

How does a sophisticated girl from New York meet and fall in love with a farm boy from Idaho? Stay tuned for the next chapter to find out this incredible story.

13

Maria's Story

Maria's and my story actually began a few years before we ever met. She was in New York and I was in Colorado. I don't know how many of you believe that some things are just meant to be. I'm not sure I even believed that until I met Maria. Some events occurred in her life before we met. After I heard the story, I certainly changed my mind. I now firmly believe in fate. The rest of this chapter will be that story. I have asked Maria to write the story, so I can include it in this book. After you read the story, I will let you decide for yourself whether you believe that some things are meant to be or not.

Here is Maria's story in her own words.

It was the summer of 1990. I was taking courses toward my master's degree. There I was, minding my own business, while unbeknownst to me, my future was an open book to her—the woman who would turn my life upside down. As I write this today, 18 years later, I can't even recall her name, but I can remember all that she said and how her words, slowly, but steadily came to life. Most vividly, I can remember all the spasms, meltdowns and emotional episodes I managed to torment myself with as a result of her uncanny presentation in my life. Dragged into this circle of torment, were those poor souls close enough to me who questioned my sanity at the time.

Before I tell this story, allow me to preface it by saying that I have *always*, since a very young age, had a steadfast belief in God. The God I believe in is ever present in my life, in *all* our lives. Sometimes we lose sight of Him or we drown out His voice with the petty chatter of mundane human nonsense. When He demands our attention, He finds a way to make Himself heard. I believe in God, in our spirit that continues beyond this earthly life, and I believe that we each hear God's call in different ways. Lastly, I *absolutely* believe that there are people who have been given special spiritual gifts to see beyond the present moment, to act as messengers, to perhaps help guide lost souls or for a higher purpose yet to be known to any of us. That said, here is my story.

I sat on one side of the classroom, initially. There was a small group of chatterers nearby and they began to grind on my nerves, so I found a seat on the opposite side of the room. There was a lady, older than myself, who often stood against the wall during lecture—she had back trouble, I later learned. We smiled cordially before and after class, exchanged pleasantries. Nothing more. One day after class, she leaned over and asked if I'd mind her confiding something to me that pertained to me. Of course, I replied, "No." I could never imagine what she was about to say!

She began, "When I look at you, I see the name Michael all around you. It's like an aura." I was a bit taken back because I had no connection to this lady, except for this class. She knew nothing about me. Michael was a fellow I dated on and off for a few months prior to this class. At the time of the class, however, we were not in contact at all. So, I responded, "Really?" She nodded then continued, "He's going to write you a letter and, later, give you a ring." I explained to her that he was a former boyfriend and the likelihood of us resuming a relationship was not very high. She disagreed. I asked her how she could be so sure of herself. She said, "It's just all around you, clear as day. I have this gift that I can see some things and your aura is very strong." Well, lucky me! I remember her smiling and asking if I wanted to know more. I was pressed for time that day, so I took a rain check on her offer for the next class. Truth be known, I was too spooked to hear more just then.

In the classes that remained, this lady proceeded to tell me that sometime in the future, I'd be involved with another man to whom she saw two women's names attached. She said one name was Frances, the other Ann. She thought perhaps it could be a love triangle she was seeing, but she wasn't sure. She just didn't know how the names related to the man, but she was sure they did. She went on to announce that I'd be moving somewhere, out of the northeastern region of the United States—didn't know where, but she said it'd be far. I adamantly disagreed, saying, "I'd *never* leave New York. My whole life is here." She adamantly disagreed with me. Then we got down to fundamentals, the alphabet. She declared the letter "D" was of very high significance in my life. Again, she couldn't pinpoint its precise meaning or relationship, but she stood by her claim that it was a *certainty* in my life.

So, the class ended. I took her phone number down and we bid each other farewell. The remainder of the summer was uneventful and, by the fall, my "freaky" lady was out of sight and out of mind. One of the eligible fellows at work had become increasingly friendly and interested in me. We knew each other by sight only, until then. He was the histology lab supervisor and I worked in the toxicology lab as a technologist at the time. He approached me one day and formally introduced himself. Shortly after that day, he asked if I'd like to have a drink, appetizers, and maybe dinner with him after work one evening. I accepted. That evening on Lake Ronkonkoma, the spark ignited, the romance took off and thus, marked the beginning of one of the most bizarre chapters of my life.

We shared a blissful three months or so and then Christmas came. Turned out, both my father and his mother were buried at St. Charles cemetery on Long Island. On Christmas morning, we decided to visit their graves and lay flowers down. We went to my father's first. When we reached his mother's tombstone, I froze in disbelief. Her name was *Frances*! I felt like I had been hit by a tidal wave. All the blood must have drained from my face. I can still remember Vin asking, "What's wrong? Are you alright?" over and over. I was very *not* ok, but I never told him why. I just said that visiting cemeteries always made me sad. Over the next few days, I decided this was just a freak coincidence. I wasn't willing to let this relationship go on account of one coincidence. And then it came to me. Wow! Vin's last name begins with a "D." Is this *The One*? Is this the Big "D?" New Year's was fabulous. The pathology department formal party was a blast. Skiing in Vermont with some of my friends was great fun. We just had some great times together.

Then, in the early spring, I sensed something wasn't right. I couldn't put my finger on it, but I felt it in my blood. One night, I had a dream. It was brief and crystal clear. Across a computer monitor, the type we had at work, I saw the name: Carol Ann Gomes. I woke up in a sweat and it never got better. That next evening after dinner at Vin's place, I asked him point blank, "Does Carol have a middle name?" He said, "Yes, why?" "What is it?" I asked, knowing what he'd say. Sure enough, he said, "It's Ann." I asked him if this former relationship was truly in the past or if it was coming back to life again. He said it wasn't like that, that he just felt sorry for her because she had so many issues, blah, blah, blah. That was all I needed to hear. It was over. He thought I was over-reacting, making a hasty decision, etc. I knew all I needed to know now. This was no longer under the category of coincidences. This was goosebumps material. The man—the two women's names—the love triangle—all of it in one neat little package. What was next?

For the remainder of that spring and part of the summer, I kept my distance from any potential love interests. For anyone who is familiar with summers on Long Island, you can appreciate how those beach clubs, those bands, those Long Island guys are more lethal than the famed Long Island Iced Tea! Nevertheless, mission accomplished.

Then, late that summer, one day, I go out to my mailbox and there's a letter in it—from my ex-boyfriend, Michael!

I simply could *not* believe my eyes. How could this lady have seen all this? Just like she predicted, he wanted me to give him one *last* chance. Now I started feeling like the undertow was pulling me in, like I had no control, no say about anything in my life. I found myself giving him that chance. Before I knew it, one night at dinner in a restaurant, the waitress delivers an engagement ring in my mousse. Great! What does a woman do when the whole restaurant is watching? I was beyond shocked, again, that undertow sucking me under. I came home, showed my mother. She was unimpressed. I was stressed. This didn't seem like a normal scenario.

The wedding date was set for December 6, 1992, over a year engagement. The anxiety and craziness that took hold of me was unlike anything I ever experienced. I felt schizophrenic. Two voices—one defending my right to follow my heart and take a different path, the other voice warning about predestiny, about how all that had been foretold was now coming to pass. I was a bonafide mess. My dearest friends tried their best to counsel me, but they themselves had never been in a position like mine. One friend said, "Don't marry him. He's not right for you. I don't care what anybody said. Don't do it." Another said, "He's a good guy. If you feel you can work your differences out, you could have a great life together." I tried my best to tempt fate, to do everything I could to sabotage my own engagement. I was aghast with my behavior and felt truly out of control.

Just a couple of months before the wedding, I dug up the lady's number and called her. I told her that things happened pretty much just as she called them. She wasn't surprised. I said, "There's just one problem. I don't feel like I love this guy." She replied, "Oh." Then she went on...she said, "I can't tell you what to do, Maria. I can only tell you what I see."

The wedding happened and I cried. I could hear Brian's words exploding in my head, "You're gonna marry this guy, Maria? It's pretty clear to me that you don't love him. What do you mean it's not that simple? It *is* that simple!" Of course, everyone thought the tears were of joy, emotional. They were emotional alright, but of emotional duress, fear that I was making the biggest mistake of my life. There it is—I married a man because I was afraid *not* to. How bizarre is that?

Within three months of being married, Michael's employer, Pall Corp., offered him a promotion as regional sales manager of a newly expanded territory, under the condition that he agree to relocate, expenses paid by Pall. Now, here's the irony. Pall is a *Long Island* based company. I was working as chemistry supervisor at a Long Island hospital at the time. I asked Michael what territory Pall had in mind. He replied, "Either Dallas or Denver." I had an immediate adverse, almost anaphylactic reaction to Dallas, so we *agreed* on Denver as the lesser of two evils. I was not happy. In fact, I came in tears and I'm still, to this very day, suffering from periodic episodes of withdrawal from my beloved New York.

During the late spring, we took a trip out to Denver for the sole purpose of fanning out my resume to line up employment in time for our move. Through his position at Pall, Michael had many influential contacts at area hospitals and the Bonfils Blood Center. We went to The Children's Hospital, Presbyterian/St. Luke's Medical Center and St. Joseph Hospital and then *he* noticed the Kaiser Permanente Franklin Medical Center, just down the block from St. Joe's. I thought it was a brokerage or something in that league, but then he said, "Well, I see people wearing lab coats. Go see if they have a lab in there." So off I go and sure as he suggested, there's a lab and I get directed to it. I left my resume with the supervisor there who told me she *knew* there'd be a position open in just about a month, right in the St. Joe's building in the emergency room lab. She said she'd forward my papers to the supervisor there and then she gave me that lady's number to call when I came back to town.

We moved the second week of June 1993. Within a week, I had the job, just like the gal at the Kaiser Franklin clinic said. Now, think about that for a minute. When was the last time anyone followed through exactly as they said they would and something important was executed without a single hitch or kink? No one grieved that an outside person was chosen for a union position. Human Resources got all my references and certifications on time. Nothing was lost. No key player was on vacation to hold things up. How commonplace is all this? *AND*... with all Michael's pull at other hospitals, I get employed by a place that neither of us had any connection to at a time when getting "into" Kaiser was supposedly quite a feat. Ok, whatever.

So, Michael was out of town way more than he was here, way more than his company initially said would be the case, and consequently, I grew accustomed to being alone most of the time. I was horribly homesick. I cannot describe the emptiness of walking around, knowing that no matter where I went, I'd *never* see a familiar face. I wasn't familiar with Target or any of the supermarket chains here. I was truly a fish out of water. One day, I asked myself as I overlooked the brown plains—no big majestic trees, no roar of the ocean, nothing but a good cup of Starbucks coffee to comfort me—"What, in the name of God, am I doing here?"

The partial answer to that question came several months later. I came over 2,000 miles to find the man I'd love forever, the one who'd be the father of my babies. We've had some bizarre connections, the most significant, of course, being *Denver*. Denver, and more specifically, me working for Kaiser, would *never* have happened if not for Michael. He led me unequivocally and absolutely to the *very* spot where I would meet my Sweetie. I've often said to Joe, "You and I are where New York and Idaho meet." Some people think we are an unusual couple because of our difference in age and where we are from. Yeah, well, my whole life is full of unusual and unlikelies. I'm still digesting alot of this and I'm not convinced this is all there is to this story. My gut instinct tells me there's more to come, more pieces to the puzzle that will answer that perennial question of what I am doing here.

In closing, I just want to express how sorry I am for any pain I caused Michael or anyone else in this ordeal. It is my sincerest hope that he found his soul mate and is happy somewhere with a family of his own. He was a good person, fun to be around and certainly deserving of love. I just wasn't capable of loving him as a husband. We weren't for each other.

14

Getting Engaged

By late summer or early fall 1994, Maria and I started seeing a lot of each other. She had separated from her first husband and was contemplating a divorce.

I started to feel like Maria was the girl I wanted to spend the rest of my life with. She was sixteen years younger than I was, but age made no difference and we were falling in love.

Her divorce became final in February 1995. I put an end to all my dating except for Maria. The more time we spent together, the more beautiful she seemed to me. There was no doubt that we had fallen deeply in love with each other. I had just turned fifty-two and she was about to turn thirty-six.

One day we were sitting in my truck and she asked me how I would feel about having children. I quickly responded by saying, "The last thing I need right now is another child." Maria didn't have any children and I saw the disappointment in her face. I quickly added, "but with the right person, I could have more children." I meant what I said and I knew she was the right person. She seemed satisfied with my response. I think I came very close to losing her at that time.

Having kids was very important to her. She was an only child and didn't want to have only one child herself. That was okay with me, but I don't think either of us could have imagined what was going to happen in the future.

In the summer of 1995, I decided to ask her to marry me. I bought an engagement ring and planned a weekend trip to San Antonio, Texas. I had been there to a Physician Assistant conference and fell in love with the river walk area of San Antonio. I told her we were going somewhere for the weekend but didn't tell her where or why. We had talked about getting engaged but had not made any definite plans. She had only told me that if we did she wanted it to be a private thing and not happen with other people around.

The river walk in San Antonio is an area where a river runs through the city. There are restaurants and shops along both sides of the river. They have boats that hold twenty to thirty people that will take you up and down the river. A guide drives the boat and points out various things of interest. It is a very romantic spot.

I made arrangements to rent a boat just for the two of us and a driver. I made reservations at one of the restaurants along the river walk. Finally, the weekend came for us to fly to San Antonio. We were soon floating down the river. I took out the ring and asked Maria to marry me. It seemed pretty private to me. Just me and Maria, the boat driver and a bottle of champaign. I was in the process of asking her to marry me and giving her the ring when we came around a bend in the river. There was an amphitheater on one side of the river and the performing stage on the other side of the river. We were now on the boat between the two. Of course, there was some big production going on at the time. The place was packed with people. When the people saw the boat with just the two of us they knew what was going on. Everyone stood up and clapped and cheered for us. So much for being a private event!

Maria accepted my proposal of marriage and we began making plans for a September 1995 wedding.

15

Marriage And Honeymoon

Maria and I were married on September 7, 1995. I was fifty-two and Maria was thirty-six. We rented the Grant-Humphreys mansion and held the wedding and reception there. The Grant-Humphreys mansion is a stately property that once served as the governor's mansion in Colorado.

Maria and me with our families at our wedding in 1995
Top row left to right: Tony (Sharon's husband), Sharon (my sister), Anne (my sister), Kent (Anne's husband)
Middle row left to right: My mother, my dad, Maria's mother
Front row left to right: Me, Maria

Maria and me in our wedding picture, 1995

We left the next day for our honeymoon. We had decided to fly to Las Vegas, Nevada and spend a couple of days there. We planned to rent a car in Las Vegas and drive to the Grand Canyon and spend a few days there before driving back to Las Vegas and flying back to Denver.

You have heard it said that opposites attract. Maria and I were opposites in many ways. One way that we were opposites is that Maria is very organized and plans every detail months in advance. I have always been one who sort of flies by the seat of my pants. I was the one in charge of making the arrangements for the honeymoon. Piece of cake! It was September and school was in session. I figured it would not be a problem to just get a motel for the night wherever we were at the end of the day. We would be near the Grand Canyon. Boy, was I wrong! We started looking for a motel about six o'clock that evening. Everywhere we stopped there were no vacancies. I, in my infinite wisdom, had not made any reservations anywhere. The Grand Canyon area was loaded with tourists from Japan, Europe, and who knows where else. There was busload after busload of tourists. Six hours later and a hundred miles from the Grand Canyon, we were totally exhausted. We had been driving since early morning. We had stopped at every motel in every town along the way. Still no vacancies. Finally we saw a motel with a vacancy sign. The town consisted of a gas station and this small motel. I have stayed in some dumpy motels in my life, but I have to say that this motel was the worst I had ever seen. The Starlight Motel almost caused the quickest marriage and divorce in history. We were so tired we decided we didn't have a choice, but to stay there. The price of the room was $19.95. That should give you a pretty good idea of what it was like. We checked in and went to our room to go to bed. There were no phones in the town that worked. Lightning had struck two weeks earlier and all the phones had been out since. We crawled into bed. The mattress was so saggy we ended up on top of each other in a valley in the middle of the mattress. Needless to say, we didn't get much sleep. When we got up in the morning, we found the bathroom sink full of various kinds of live bugs. There were all kinds of bugs that I had never seen before. We decided to shower and get the heck out of there. When we turned on the shower, all that came out was little more than a drip of ugly brownish water. We got out of there as fast as we could. Maria still has the receipt from that motel. I think she is just waiting for the right time to pull it out and use it against me somehow.

A year after we were married, we decided to start our family. It was a very simple idea that turned into a nightmare for us. About the same time, I began having problems with my back and my previously injured knee. I was in so much pain from my back and knee that I couldn't work. I went to see an orthopedic surgeon. After looking at the X-rays and examining my knee, we decided it was time for a total knee replacement. We scheduled the surgery for September of 1996. I also saw a neurosurgeon about my back. I needed surgery on my back also. The orthopedic surgeon and neurosurgeon got together to decide which one should be done first. They thought if I had my knee replaced first that my back would get better. They felt that my knee might have been the cause of my back pain because my knee was bowing out so much it was putting a strain on my back. In the meantime, I was sent home on Percocet and Valium. I was pretty much in bed all the time. Getting out of bed to go to the bathroom was an excruciating experience even while I was taking the medicine. Valium is a medicine that has an amnesiac effect; it makes you forget what is going on. The first time I ran out of medicine I had Maria get a refill from my doctor. She told him that I was still in a lot of pain. He doubled the strength of the Valium. I continued to take the same number of pills that I had been taking, not remembering the strength was doubled. I also had trouble remembering when I took the last pills and I sort of took too much medicine too often. One evening Maria came home from work and I was nearly comatose. She dragged me down the stairs, put me in the car, and took me to the emergency room. I was admitted to the hospital and stayed there for a week. To this day, I do not remember hardly anything about that week. I developed pneumonia while I was in the hospital. They tell me I came very close to dying. I do recall one or two incidents during that week. I was lying in bed and all of a sudden I had to go to the bathroom. I jumped out of bed to go, but I was so weak and dizzy and confused that I fell onto the patient who was in the bed next to me. The next thing I knew, I was back in my bed, tied to the bed by my hands and feet.

Maria was very worried about me during this time. She was at the hospital before she went to work in the mornings, during her breaks, during her lunch hour, after work and then again after supper until they chased her out of the hospital at night. One day she came to the hospital and it looked like no one had even been in to see if I needed anything. My water pitcher was empty and had been since she left the night before. Maria was immediately all over the staff like a chicken on a june bug. I never had an empty water pitcher after that.

My sister called me at the hospital one day to see how I was doing. Maria was at work at the time. I answered the phone and began to talk to her. I was so groggy and out of it that she couldn't make any sense of what I was saying. She asked if Maria was there so she could talk to someone she could understand. I said, "No, I haven't seen her for days." That was anything but the truth, but I am sure my sister wondered what kind of woman I had married.

I finally got out of the hospital and was doing much better. Maria took my pills away and gave them to me appropriately. A few weeks later, it was time for my knee replacement surgery. I had the surgery in early September 1996. It is very important to do rehabilitation after knee replacement surgery. My back was still so painful I couldn't get up to rehabilitate my knee. Twenty days later, I went back into the hospital and had surgery on my back. That surgery was very successful and my back pain disappeared. I was able to rehab my knee and my back got better and better.

Two months later, I went back to work feeling better than I had for a long time.

During this time, we were trying to get pregnant. We tried for six months without success. We went to an infertility specialist. He worked with us for another six months. We tried everything that he knew how to do, but still were unable to get pregnant. He finally referred us to Dr. William Schoolcraft. He is a nationally know guru of *in vitro* fertilization. After an initial consultation, we decided to give it one more try.

Our decision to go ahead with *in vitro* fertilization started us on a bumpy roller coaster ride for the next year. First came the battery of lab tests and the exams. The exam revealed a slight problem that could easily be remedied by some minor surgery. When that was completed, it was time for Maria to begin her regimen of medications. Basically, Dr. Schoolcraft took over the reproductive functioning of Maria's body. Included in the medication regimen was an injection that she needed every day. It wasn't very long before she had a very sore and bruised rear end.

We finally finished with the medication portion of the process and it was time for the next step. Part of the medication process was to stimulate the ovaries to produce as many eggs as possible.

The egg retrieval process required an ultrasound machine, a very long needle with a test tube attached to one end. I will leave the rest to your imagination. Dr. Schoolcraft was able to retrieve eight eggs from this procedure.

The next step in the process was to fertilize the eggs in the lab. When this step was completed, the fertilized eggs were watched under the microscope to see which ones were progressing the best. On the third day after fertilization, it was time to re-implant the fertilized eggs into Maria's uterus. Dr. Schoolcraft told us that four fertilized eggs was the maximum he would re-implant. We could choose any number up to four. He told us the statistics of his practice: 75% chance of having one child; 25% chance of having twins; and less than 5% chance of having triplets. We didn't even want to know about the chances of having quadruplets. As I mentioned earlier, Maria was an only child and she didn't want to have only one child. We opted to re-implant four eggs and see what happened. Dr. Schoolcraft explained another very interesting thing to us. He told us that as women get older, their eggs get harder. They can get fertilized, but the problem comes when they attach to the uterus the eggshells are too hard for the egg to break out and begin growing. Dr. Schoolcraft had solved this problem by carefully cracking the eggshells before they were re-implanted.

The four fertilized eggs were re-implanted on the third day. Now, all we could do was wait and see what happened. We were told to get a pregnancy test in ten days. We had the test done in ten days and, when it turned positive, we were very excited.

There are two types of pregnancy tests. The one we had done is called a qualitative pregnancy test. It simply tells you whether you are pregnant or not. The other type is called a quantitative pregnancy test. It measures a pregnancy hormone call HCG and tells you how pregnant you are. The longer you are pregnant the higher the HCG amount. It is not an exact test, but gives you some idea of how many weeks pregnant you are. We followed up the original pregnancy test with this test. The amount of HCG that showed on this test was extremely high for the length of time Maria had been pregnant. We learned from this test that she was pregnant with more than one baby.

Two weeks later, it was time for an ultrasound to see what we had. As the ultrasound was being done, the tech said, "There's one." After looking around a bit more she said, "There's two." We were extremely happy with the news. She looked around a little more and said, "Oh look, there's a third one." At this point, both Maria and I started crying. I'm not sure why. Probably because the thought of having triplets was pretty overwhelming. We had been hoping for twins and weren't sure how we felt about the bonus.

Dr. Schoolcraft had done his job. It was time for us to go see a high risk OB/GYN doctor. Dr. McDuffie was now the doctor who was going to take care of us through the rest of the pregnancy. We had frequent visits with him and many ultra sounds. When it became apparent where the babies were located, they were named Baby A, Baby B, and Baby C. They were all doing well.

An amniocentesis was done. Actually, three amnioceteses were done at the same time, one for each baby. The amnio fluid from each sac was sent to the lab for analysis. This revealed that all three were genetically okay. There were no problems with genetic disorders. We also learned that we were going to have one boy and two girls.

After some discussion, we chose names for each of the babies. Our son would be named Joseph Paul. Joseph after his grandfather on my side of the family and, of course, after me, also. Paul, after his grandfather on Maria's side of the family. Amanda Adele. Adele is Maria's mother's name. Sara June. June is my mother's name. So, we were able to include the names of all four grandparents in naming the triplets.

Dr. McDuffie also told us that with triplets, it was inevitable that they would be born early. He told us that at some point Maria would develop pre-eclampsia. This is a condition that can develop during pregnancy. The only treatment is to deliver the babies. Dr. McDuffie's job was to try to prevent this from occurring as long as possible.

To make things even more interesting and stressful, during the time we were going through the *in vitro* process, my daughter, Lori, became pregnant with her fourth child. My son, Jason, and his wife also became pregnant. Everyone was due during the first five months of 1998.

16

Birth Of Triplets

Without a doubt, 1998 was the happiest, yet most difficult year, I had faced in my life. On my 55th birthday, January 27th, my daughter, Lori, presented me with my fourth grandchild, a granddaughter named Kira.

Maria and I lived in a house in the Capitol Hill area of Denver. Our house was on the corner of one of the busiest streets in the city. We decided that it was not a good idea to try and raise triplets on that busy intersection. We sold the house and bought a new home in the north suburbs of Denver. We moved into the new home in early February. It was a difficult move because Maria was six months pregnant and, as you can imagine, had a rather large stomach. I remember going out to eat and making many waitresses nervous that Maria was going to go into labor any second. They always asked when she was due. When she told them she was not due until May, they couldn't believe their eyes and ears.

A normal pregnancy lasts about forty weeks. When Maria was twenty-eight weeks along, Dr. McDuffie ordered bed rest for her until she delivered. It was near the end of February when she was ordered to bed. She spent most of her time lying down, but it was hard to keep her down. She was trying to get everything ready for the babies when they came home. A visiting nurse came every Friday to check her condition. She did well for the next four weeks, but by the end of March, Maria developed pre-eclampsia and was admitted to the hospital. Maria was thirty-two-and-a-half weeks along and arrangements were made to deliver the babies as soon as possible. Maria was wheeled into the delivery room in the evening of March 30, 1998. The delivery room was like a circus. There were fifteen or twenty people all hurrying around getting ready to do their jobs. There were three incubators lined up against the wall. Each incubator had its own neonatology team to take care of one of the babies. Finally, everyone was ready and the delivery proceeded. Joseph Paul was born first. He weighed four pounds and four ounces. One minute later, Amanda Adele was born. She weighed three pounds and eight ounces. One minute after that, Sara June was born. She weighed a whopping two pounds and fourteen ounces. It all happened so fast that it was really mind-boggling. The initial care of the babies was completed in the delivery room and then they were whisked off to the Neonatal Intensive Care Unit. Maria was taken to her room. I went into the NICU and just stood there with my mouth open in disbelief. I saw one of the OB/GYN doctors that I knew from work and told him that we had just had triplets. He told me something that turned out to be very prophetic. He said, "One plus one plus one does not equal three." Boy was he right!

Six weeks later, my son Jason and his wife had my fifth grandchild. A grandson, named Hayden, was born on May 17th, 1998. In a period of three and a half months, I had become the father of three children and the grandfather of two more children.

Maria was released from the hospital and we had to go home without our babies. They were too premature and too small to go home just yet. They were expected to stay in the NICU for about a month. Premature babies are at risk for many problems, so we were not out of the woods yet. We made several trips to the hospital every day to help take care of the babies. We held them, and loved them, and anxiously awaited the day when we could bring them home. They were doing very well for about a week and then the trouble started. One morning, we arrived at the hospital and met with the neonatologist. He said that Joe had a bloody stool during the night. An X-ray was done and it confirmed that he had developed necrotizing enterocolitis (NEC). NEC is a disorder of the intestinal tract. It is seen mostly in premature infants. It is a very serious problem. Twenty-five percent of the premature infants who get NEC end up dying. You can imagine the anxiety that caused us. I'm happy to say he survived the treatment and has had no lasting effects from the condition.

Amanda developed a problem that caused her stomach to fill up with air. They had to repeatedly put a tube down her throat into her stomach to let the air out. She had trouble eating. The doctors figured out she had reflux that was causing her pain when she ate. She was a very cranky baby for a long time.

Sara had a different problem. Her heart rate would drop to a very low rate and she would stop breathing for a length of time. She would start breathing again after the monitor would go off and someone would shake her a little to stimulate her.

All three had a different problem and they kept us very concerned throughout their stay in the NICU. They all received excellent care while they were there. In preparation for coming home, they were taken out of the incubators and all put in one bed together. The neonatologist told us they were going to put Sara in the middle. She was the smallest and needed the warmth from the other two. The next time we came to the hospital to see them, Sara was on the end and not in the middle. Amanda was in the middle. We asked the neonatologist about it. We said, "We thought you were going to put Sara in the middle." He said, "Yes, that is correct." Maria said, "That is not Sara in the middle." He said, "Are you sure?" It was a very funny conversation and no harm done.

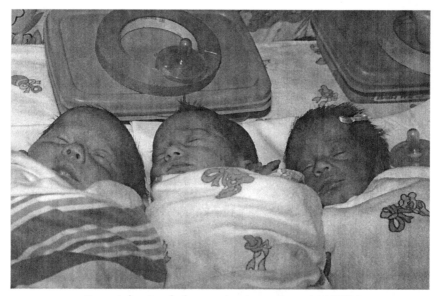

Our triplets just before coming home from the NICU
Left to right: Joe, Amanda, Sara in April 1998

Finally, it was time for them to start coming home. Amanda was the first one to come home. She had been home for about five hours when she had a bloody stool. We took her back to the NICU. An X-ray confirmed she had developed NEC and she was readmitted to the NICU where she stayed receiving treatment for the next ten days.

A few days after Amanda went back into the hospital, Joe was able to come home. A week later, Amanda came home. Sara was still there. The NICU rule was that she had to go three days without having an episode of low heart rate and stopping breathing. She would get close to the three-day mark and then would have another episode. The three days would start over again. It was a very trying time having two at home and one still in the hospital. We finally convinced them to let

Sara come home with a heart and respiratory monitor. They allowed that to happen because Maria and I were both medically trained and knew what to do if problems occurred. We finally had all of our babies home, and we began the process of raising triplets.

17

The Triplets' Early Years

I had this silly notion that once we got the triplets home that life would be much easier. No more running back and forth to the hospital. No more having some home and some in the hospital. They were all right here at home for us to take care of and love to pieces.

Their first night at home was not a night at all. It was a nightmare. The monitor we had for Sara arrived, and they showed us how to hook it up to her. It consisted of a belt that went around her chest with snap on wires that led to the monitor. If her heart rate or breathing dropped below a set level, alarms would go off. The alarms went off about forty times the first night. Every time they would go off, we would rush to her room and gently shake her to stimulate her heart and breathing. She would wake up and look at us like, "What are you doing? Why don't you let me sleep?" Every time the alarm went off, it scared us to death. She was always fine when we checked on her. We finally figured out the next day that the monitor was faulty. It would just go off for no apparent reason.

We had all three of the babies in the same room, but each in their own crib. We were fortunate to be able to take time off work in the beginning. Maria took six months and I was able to take three weeks off. Trying to keep track of who ate when, how much, who pooped, and who had their diapers changed became a nightmare. We finally made a white board to help keep track of all this.

When they first got home, they were eating two ounces of formula every three hours. Being preemies, they were not real good at sucking down the formula. It took about thirty minutes for each one to eat the two ounces of formula. By the time we would prepare the formula, change the diapers, and get them fed was about two-and-a-half hours. Another half-hour and it was time to start the process all over again. Maria and I took turns feeding and changing them. While one was feeding them the other would be trying to get a few hours of sleep. We barely got out of bed for three weeks, other than to feed them, and occasionally grab a bite to eat. We were totally exhausted all the time.

Things started to get better as time went on. They were eating more with each feeding and eating a little less often. Life was returning to some semblance of normalcy. I went back to work while Maria wrestled with the three of them all day while I was gone. I remember coming home from work and finding the babies sleeping, and Maria out like a light on the bed. They all had colic late in the afternoon, and were absolutely terrible for three hours every day before I got home. By that time Maria was exhausted, and usually wasn't in a very good mood. I had the easiest part of the job. I got to go to work every day.

Then the real trouble started. Amanda stopped eating. Every time she would try to eat she would cry like she was in pain. She was so small, it didn't take long for her to get dehydrated. I took her to the doctor. She was admitted to the hospital for IV fluids and to figure out what was wrong. I stayed at the hospital with her while Maria stayed home with the other two. The doctors figured out that she had reflux (heartburn), and put her on some medicine. We came home from the hospital, and she did pretty well on the medicine for a while.

Sara had the next problem. She got sick and was running a fever of 102 degrees. She was two months old, but adjusting her age for her prematurity, she was really the age of a normal newborn full-term baby. A fever in this age group is very concerning. She was admitted to the hospital and got a full septic workup. Spinal tap, blood cultures, blood work, IV antibiotics, chest X-ray, and urinalysis. She was in the hospital for two days. I stayed there with her while Maria stayed home with the other two. All the tests came back normal, and it was decided she had a virus and would be okay. We had no outside help, so these times were very difficult for us.

Soon after Sara got home, Amanda stopped eating again. She became dehydrated and ended up in the hospital again. The medicine they had given her had stopped working and her reflux was back worse than ever. Again, I stayed in the hospital with Amanda, and Maria was home with the other two. Fortunately, my parents had come from

Idaho to see the kids and spend a few days with us. Early the next morning, after Amanda had been admitted to the hospital, I got a call from Maria. She was downstairs in the emergency room with Joe. He had developed an inguinal hernia that had become incarcerated (stuck), and needed to have surgery to fix the problem. So, here I was, upstairs in the hospital with Amanda, Maria is downstairs with Joe in the emergency room getting ready to go to surgery. My parents are home taking care of Sara. Just an example of how sometimes the logistics of having triplets can be somewhat overwhelming. This all occurred within four months of the triplets coming home from the hospital.

They changed Amanda's medicine, Joe came home from the surgery, Amanda came home, and we had a relatively uneventful rest of their first year of life. One incident that really stands out in my mind, however, is near their first birthday when a stomach virus invaded our house. All three of them had two days of vomiting and diarrhea. I have never seen so much poop and puke in my life. We all survived that episode somehow.

Our triplets and my two grandchildren, all born in 1998. They were all one-year-olds when this photo was taken
Left to right: Kira (my granddaughter), Joe (my son), Sara (my daughter), Amanda (my daughter), Hayden (my grandson)

Things went along very well until they were nearly five. They all started having trouble with their tonsils. They all developed such large tonsils that they were having trouble swallowing, and were all snoring very loudly at night. Over the next few months, they all had their tonsils removed and things were going well again. Except for being exhaustingly busy all the time, life was very good.

Amanda had developed an umbilical hernia while she was still an infant. They usually give them until about five or six years of age to heal on their own. If that doesn't happen, then they are surgically repaired. Amanda's didn't heal, so it was back to the operating room to repair her umbilical hernia.

We had finally made it to the time when the triplets would be starting kindergarten. At least now, we would have a few hours a day together, without children, when we could relax a little.

Our triplets off to school
Left to right: Amanda, Sara, Joe

18

SOME THINGS ALONG THE WAY

I am sure God must have known how difficult raising triplets is. I think that is why he gave them all a sense of humor. They are extremely funny. I know they don't have any idea how funny they are. I also know that at times their funniness is the only thing that has saved them. What follows are a few examples of many hilarious things they have said and done.

When the triplets became mobile, we noticed that they tended to move around the house as a group. Where you would find one you would find them all. We also noticed that they were very competitive. They were always trying to outdo each other. The competitiveness has gotten worse as they have gotten older. They each spend a great amount of energy making sure one doesn't get more gifts at birthdays and Christmas. They are also very competitive about the grades they get in school.

Sensory integration disorder is a condition that is common in premature infants. It simply means that those with this condition have trouble processing certain stimuli. Of course, all three of our triplets had this condition.

It took a long time before any of them would put their bare feet onto the grass. We would try to put them on the grass. As soon as their feet touched the grass, they would pull their feet up and cry or whine.

One of the most difficult transitions we had to make, was getting them off baby food and onto table food. There were certain foods they couldn't stand to have in their mouths because of the texture of the food. It took them a long time to overcome this.

They also couldn't stand to have anything on their hands. If they would get food, or some other substance, on their hands they would hold their hands up in the air and cry until we got their hands cleaned up.

Being around groups of people set them off. They would become very withdrawn and cranky if there were too many people around.

Loud noises upset them greatly. I remember a couple of times when they would be upstairs, asleep for the night, and we would be cooking supper. We would be cooking some meat in the oven. A few times, enough smoke would come out of the oven when we opened the oven door, to set off the smoke alarms. Instead of three sleeping babies, we had three babies standing up in their cribs screaming at the top of their lungs. It would take quite a while to get them all calmed down and back to sleep again.

Sara, the youngest and smallest at birth, seemed to progress more rapidly than the other two. She was always the first to master new tasks. She was very focused on what she was doing. She became known as the little adult. We often referred to her as an adult born in a child's body. We would tell her that she could grow up to be the first woman president of the United States. She was always excited about that. One evening at supper, we mentioned again about her being president. She said, "No, I don't want to be president," and began crying. She was four years old at the time, and we had recently returned from a road trip to South Dakota, Mt. Rushmore, and Yellowstone Park. We were very surprised at her negative reaction to becoming president. We quizzed her about her reaction. She simply said, "I don't want to be president because I don't want them to cut off my head and put it on that mountain."

One evening, Sara and I were sitting on the couch. Sara was five. All of a sudden, Sara started crying hysterically. She had some blood coming out of her mouth. I couldn't figure out what had happened. She had just been sitting there. She held out her hand and there was a tooth in her hand with some blood on it. All of the kids had some loose teeth and we had warned them that soon those teeth would be coming out. The warning evidently didn't do any good. When Amanda saw Sara's tooth had come out, she started screaming at me, "Put it back. Put it back."

Whenever Maria or I would discipline Joe or Amanda that became Sara's cue to chime in and chastise them right along with Maria and I. One evening, while Maria was working, I had fixed supper for the kids. Joe and Amanda were fooling around instead of eating. Sara began telling them how childish they were and that they should grow up a little. Joe said, "Why does Sara always have to act like a little adult?" Sara said matter of factly, "I am just trying to take responsibility for the house the way Mom does when she is home."

When the triplets were in the fourth grade, I would walk them to school in the mornings. As usual, Joe and Amanda would get way ahead of Sara and I. They would start fooling around by getting off the sidewalk onto the edge of the road. I had yelled at them a couple of times to slow down and stay on the sidewalk. Sara then decided to take charge and began yelling at them to get back on the sidewalk and slow down. She then looked up at me and asked, "Do you think I will make a good mom when I grow up?"

Amanda has a little natural curl to her hair. The girls liked to have their hair braided. When the braids were taken out, Amanda's hair was very wavy. One day, after the braids were taken out, Sara came to Maria and said, "Um."

Whenever Sara started a sentence with "um" you knew you were in for a classic statement. Sara said, "Um, Amanda's hair looks like Jesus."

One evening, when I was getting ready to fix supper for the kids, I couldn't get them to agree on anything they wanted to eat. The harder I tried the worse it got. Finally, I had reached the end of my rope and I told them, "You are on your own. You get your own supper." I thought that might get them to agree on something. Instead, Amanda and Sara got up and fixed supper for everyone, and also packed all their lunches for the next day at school. So much for using that technique to try to get them to agree on something.

One day, Maria was having a discussion with the triplets. They had just come home from religion class and were talking about St. Francis of Assisi. Amanda asked, "Why do they call him a sissy?"

A couple of years ago, Maria developed a corn on her second toe. It kept getting larger and more painful. We had used some medicine for corns, but it just kept getting bigger and more painful. We were getting ready to go on vacation, and were going to be doing a lot of walking. My expertise was in trauma and urgent care. I hadn't dealt with corns during my career, but I decided that I could take care of it. I gathered all the stuff I needed and was ready to shave the corn down so it wouldn't be so painful. I numbed up Maria's toe and began shaving the corn down with a scalpel. Of course, I had three sets of wide eyes watching my every move. Maria asked me how deep I was going to go. I said, "I didn't know for sure, because I had never actually done this before." Maria then asked me if she should continue to use the medicine. I said, "That would probably be a good idea." About that time, I shaved down far enough to get into some normal tissue and it bled a little. I told Maria it probably wouldn't be a good idea to use the medicine for a few days, because it would probably sting. It was at this moment, that suddenly I was no longer Amanda's dad. She took Maria by the hand, looked her straight in the eye, and said, "The man has no idea what he is doing."

Joe has his own brand of humor. One Mother's Day, we were going out to lunch. I usually dress in Levi's, and a t-shirt and sneakers when I am around the house. I had dressed up in slacks, a dress shirt and regular shoes for the Mother's Day lunch. When I came downstairs, Joe was sitting on the couch. He said, "Wow Dad! I've never seen you accessorize like that."

One Labor Day, I was working, and I got a call from Maria. She had taken the kids bike riding and had lacerated her ankle on the bike chain. I told her I was just getting off work but, if she would come to the clinic, I would stay and sew her ankle up. I was waiting for them in the lobby when they arrived. I had on my white lab coat and scrubs. I walked toward them to greet them when Joe said, "Why do you walk like that?" I said, "Walk like what?" Joe said, "Like you are all important or something."

Joe once said about his sister Amanda: "She's cute, but she is evil."

It is our routine, in the mornings, for me to fix breakfast while Maria gets their clothes ready for school. We have the TV on The Weather Channel so we know how to dress them for school. One particular day, the TV said it was going to be a high of forty degrees. Joe asked me, "Dad, using similes and metaphors, tell me what forty degrees is like."

There are many more things I could tell about but this should give you some idea why I spend most of my time laughing.

19

Losing My Dad

In January 2003, I turned sixty years old. It was like the day I turned sixty, someone flipped a switch and things started going wrong with me. I developed high blood pressure. My cholesterol became elevated and I developed a mild case of diabetes. My morning routine changed. I now had to take a handful of pills every morning just to get my day started. I would take my pills, look in the mirror and say, "Oh well, live better chemically."

My back started bothering me again about that same time. It became progressively worse and soon the pain was radiating down both my legs. I finally gave in, and went to see the neurosurgeon. He did an MRI, and discovered I had a condition called spondylothesis. Simply, one of my vertebrae had slipped out of place. I needed surgery to fix the problem. I needed a fusion and some metal put in my back to stabilize the vertebrae.

The surgery was done the first week of July. I spent five days in the hospital. It was an extremely painful surgery. I had been home from the hospital for two days. We decided to call my parents in Idaho and let them know how I was doing. We called about 7 pm and talked for about a half hour. All five of us spoke with my father. That was unusual because usually the kids were off playing somewhere and didn't get on the phone. I remember my dad telling me how bad he felt that day. I remember saying to him, "You can't expect to feel like you did when you were twenty. You are almost eighty-four." He said, "The way I feel today I will never see eighty-four." We finished our conversation and went about our nightly routine. We put the kids to bed, and Maria and I went to bed about 10:30 pm. At 11:00 pm, the phone rang. It was my mother. She told me that my dad had gone to bed about 9:00 pm, and she a little later. She tried to talk to him for a minute, but he didn't respond. She then realized that he had died in his sleep before she went to bed. He was just a few days away from his eighty-fourth birthday.

His death affected me greatly. I hardly slept that night. Early the next morning, Maria loaded up the car, and we headed for Idaho some five-hundred-fifty miles away. I couldn't help Maria at all. She loaded the car, and kids, and drove us all the way to Idaho. After the funeral, she loaded everything up, and drove us all the way back to Denver.

The trip to and from Idaho was extremely painful because of the recent back surgery. I couldn't find a comfortable position. It was pure agony. As painful as my back was, it couldn't hold a candle to the pain in my heart. I had just lost my best friend, my father.

After the funeral service, we went to the cemetery for the graveside services. Part of the graveside service included a twenty-one-gun salute, because my dad was a veteran. The triplets were five-years-old, but still had some problems with the sensory integration disorder. We were concerned about the noise the guns would make when they were fired. We gathered the kids near us and explained to them that there was going to be a loud noise, but it was okay. When the guns were fired, we had three kids screaming and crying at the top of their lungs.

Maria wrote a poem about my father from the triplets' point of view. She framed it and it is surrounded by pictures of my father with each of the kids. The pictures she added around the poem made an incredible memorial. Even though you won't be able to get the full effect that the pictures add, I wanted to include the poem in this chapter.

Grandpa, Don't Forget Me

Grandpa, don't forget me
As you walk into the light.
I'm still little and now you've gone
somewhere out of sight.

They tell me someday

we'll see each other again,

so Grandpa, don't forget me,

up there in heaven.

I want to always remember you

as a jolly, old fella,

sittin' in your favorite chair, watching TV

and talkin' about "Pocatella."

Playing the piano, while Grandma sang

Grandpa, why did you go?

So suddenly and forever?

There's so much I still don't know.

They say you are in heaven now,

where all good people are.

Together with God and the angels.

Grandpa is it far?

Can you really see me now

although we are apart?

Do you know how much I loved you

with my little heart?

And do you know that we're a part of each other?

this, Mama says is true.

So, Grandpa, don't forget me up there,

and I promise I won't forget you.

Left to right: My sister Anne, my dad (twelve years before his death), my mom, my sister Sharon and me at my parents' 50th wedding anniversary

A couple of months after the funeral, things had returned to normal. I had recovered from my back surgery, and returned to work. The triplets had started kindergarten, and we were back into a routine.

I was working three twelve-hour shifts a week at this time. Eleven am until eleven pm. One evening back in 2001, I received a call from

Maria about 9:00 pm. We have some friends who live just down the block from us. Brett and Cheri King. They have a set of twin boys, Devin and Brady. They are the same age as our triplets. It seems that Devin had dove headfirst out of the bathtub and hit his head on the toilet leaving him with a laceration over his right eyebrow. I called them. They described the cut to me to see if I thought they needed to take him to the emergency room for stitches. It sounded like the laceration needed stitches, so I offered to come by their house after I got off work. I told them I could sew it up at their house, if they wanted me to. They agreed, so I gathered everything I needed, and went to their house after I got off work. Devin was asleep by the time I arrived. We laid him on the dining room table, and I got everything ready to go. I asked Brett and Cheri to hold him, because I was afraid he would wake up when I numbed up the laceration. That usually stings a lot. I got him numbed up, and he didn't even move, let alone wake up. Brett asked me if they still needed to hold him. I said, "I didn't think so." Brett asked me if it was okay if he videotaped me sewing up Devin. I said, "Yes, as long as you don't use the video against me in court." We all laughed, and Brett videotaped me sewing Devin's laceration. Devin didn't wake up, and when we were finished they put him to bed. He didn't even realize what had happened to him until the next morning when he woke up and Brett and Cheri showed him his stitches.

20

Retirement

In September 2004, my son Jason and his wife presented me with my sixth grandchild. A little girl named Presley.

I turned sixty-two a few months later, January 2005. I had now reached the age when I could take early retirement. I could collect a pension from Kaiser and receive Social Security benefits. I discovered, at this time, that each of the triplets would receive a Social Security benefit also because they were my minor children. I figured out that between my pension from Kaiser and the benefits we would get from Social Security, I would be getting close to what I was making working full time. I could easily make up the difference by working two or three shifts a month.

After taking everything into consideration, I decided to take early retirement. Maria would continue to work half time. There is a federal rule that if you retire from a company and start taking your pension, you cannot work for that company again for six months. I decided to take the six months off and not seek employment elsewhere. At the end of the six-month period, I applied for an on call position with Kaiser. I was rehired and began working a few shifts a month for Kaiser. It was a nice feeling to be able to work when I wanted.

I was home a lot more and could spend a lot more time with the triplets and Maria. I was around enough to take some of the load off Maria. That load was, and still is tremendous. She works half time, takes care of a very active set of triplets, and takes care of her elderly mother. Her mother lives by herself in an apartment near our home.

She doesn't drive, so Maria has to take her shopping, to her doctor appointments, and make sure she is taking her medications properly. I was glad to be home more to help her with some of these things.

We were able to take some long road trips. The last one we took lasted three weeks and covered over five thousand miles. We drove from Denver to New York. New York to Florida. Florida to Denver. It was a fantastic three weeks.

In September 2007, my son Jason and his wife presented me with my seventh grandchild. His name is Rylan.

In January 2008, I turned sixty-five. The triplets turned ten in March 2008, and are just finishing the fourth grade.

Jason and his family live just a few miles from us. Lori and her family live in Fort Collins, Colorado about forty miles from us.

Maria's mom is in a nursing home near us. She is there rehabilitating from a bad bout with her asthma and Influenza B. She was extremely ill for two weeks and we didn't think she was going to survive. Survive she did, and is doing much better. We expect to be able to move her to an assisted living center soon.

We get together often with Lori and Jason and their families to celebrate birthdays and holidays. It is nice that we are all close enough to be able to do this.

21

Reflections

Writing this book has been a wonderful and melancholic experience for me. It has allowed me, in a way, to relive the best of times, and the worst of times, as I recalled in great detail the events of my life. I believe that everyone, at some point, should write their life story for their posterity to enjoy.

I have never been a great motivator. I do not preach to anyone about what they should or shouldn't do. I just hope that by reading this book that someone may find the courage and motivation to go after a life long dream. I am living proof that it can be done, and that you are never too old to accomplish it.

My parents

I am grateful to have been raised by good and honorable parents. They taught me how to be a good person. They taught me how to work hard, always do my best, and be honest in dealing with others. They taught me to be respectful of other people, and to obey the laws of the land. Then they showed me, by their example, how it should be done.

Maria

What can you say about the woman who has spent the last thirteen years trying to save me from myself? I am very fortunate to have her as my wife. Her love for me has shown me, for the first time in my life, what true unselfish love is. If you are fortunate enough to experience that kind of love, you will know it, and understand what I mean. I love her with all my heart.

She is a magnificent mother to my triplets. She is the epitome of "a mother's love."

I only hope she knows how thankful I am for all she has done for our children and me.

Lori

My firstborn child. I want to thank you for the love you have shown me throughout the years. Your life has brought me much joy and happiness. I am very proud of you. You have accomplished a lot in your life, and have raised a wonderful family. I am sorry for the times that were very difficult for me, and I wasn't able to provide for you the way I would have liked. Just know I love you very much.

My daughter Lori and her husband Kurt in 2008

Lori's children in 2008
Left to right: Chase, Kira, Jamie, Colin

JASON

I want to apologize to you for not always being there for you when I should have been. You were the unfortunate one who had to bear the brunt of some very difficult times in my life. I know it was hard for you because you were at the age when you needed me a lot. I know I wasn't always there for you. In spite of all that, you have done very well for yourself. I am very proud of you for what you have accomplished, and the wonderful family you have raised. I have always been a little jealous, but proud, of your musical talent. I have always wanted to have that musical talent. You, more than most, know how little musical talent I have.

You are a kind loving person, and I am thankful to you for the love you have shown me during your life.

*Jason's Family in 2008
Jason holding Presley, Hayden seated in the middle,
Nicole holding Rylan*

LITTLE JOE

It is amazing how much joy and happiness you have brought to me during your short ten years of life. You are such a loving person. It makes me very proud to be your father. You are a very intelligent young man. You have an amazing amount of talent. You will be able to accomplish anything you want, if you put your mind to it. I want you to always make good choices in your life. Making bad choices will be the only thing that can prevent you from being successful in anything you choose to undertake. I love you with all my heart and want only the very best for you.

Amanda

You are my loving little "Mooshie." I know your heart is just spilling over with love. You are a beautiful young lady. I am very proud to be your father. You have made my life a very happy one. You are very smart. You can be whatever you want to be. You also have a competitive streak like I have never seen before. It is this competitiveness that will allow you to succeed in anything you attempt. You just have to learn to control it so it can work to your advantage and not get you into trouble. I love you very much and want you to have a happy and prosperous life.

Sara

My soft-hearted "Peanut." You are my youngest child. I am very proud to be your father. You make me very happy. You are a very bright young lady. You have the ability to be anything you want to be, or do anything you want to do. You are my little adult. It is okay to be a little adult, but don't forget you are still a child. Spend your time being a child while you are one. There is plenty of time to be an adult later. I love you very much and my hopes for you are to be happy and successful in your life.

Triplets

It is sometimes difficult for me to look at you guys as individuals. The temptation is to look at you and treat you as a group. I know you are each unique individuals. I love you all very much. Each in a different way, but not one more than the other. I hope you remain as close to each other, throughout your lives, as you are now.

My wife Maria, me and our triplets
Left to right: Amanda, Joe, Sara

GRANDKIDS

Jamie, Chase, Colin, Kira, Hayden, Presley and Rylan. I love each and every one of you with all my heart. You all have made me very happy and proud. It is a medical fact that the seven of you will be my only grandchildren for a long time. I won't have anymore until the triplets grow up and begin having children of their own.

To My Unborn Grandchildren

You will be the child of one of my triplets. I only hope that God will grant me a long and healthy life so that I am around to see you come into this world. I do not know what kind of world it will be by the time you are born. I worry about that a lot. I do know that you will have wonderful parents.

If I do not have the privilege of being here when you are born, I hope this book will allow you to know about me, who I am, and where you came from.

I am sixty-five years old as I finish this book. I am very content and happy with my life. I am still working, doing what I love to do. I am healthy. I have a wonderful wife. I have five beautiful children. I have seven awesome grandchildren. I have time to enjoy it all. Life is so good!

About The Author

Joe Rowsell was born and raised in rural southeast Idaho. He lived in several places throughout the United States while working for the Thom McAn shoe company.

In 1971, Joe moved to Denver, Colorado. Two years later, he began a real-estate career in the Denver metropolitan area.

After nearly a decade in real estate, Joe reached a turning point in his life when he decided to return to college in 1985. He earned a master's degree in medical science from the University of Colorado in 1988. That same year, he began a career as a physician assistant at St. Joseph Hospital in Denver.

Joe Rowsell retired from Kaiser Permanente in 2005. He currently lives in the Denver area and continues to work part time as a physician assistant for Kaiser Permanente.